Sunset

Landscaping
for
Small Spaces

By the Editors of Sunset Books and Sunset Magazine

Muted colors set a quiet mood for a small garden.
Design: Konrad Gauder/Landsculpture.

Sunset Publishing Corporation ■ Menlo Park, California

Book Editor
Phyllis Elving

Research & Text
Cynthia Overbeck Bix
Philip Edinger
Susan Lang
Susan Warton

Coordinating Editors
Deborah Thomas Kramer
Suzanne Normand Mathison

Design
Joe di Chiarro

Illustrations
Lois Lovejoy

Editorial Director, Sunset Books:
Bob Doyle

Fifth printing November 1996

When space is at a premium, you can create room for plants by gardening upward—on fences, walls, trellises.

Small Pleasures

It's been said that the best things come in small packages. Perhaps nothing demonstrates that idea better than the small garden. While the image of a wide lawn or woodsy acre is appealing, a small garden has a charm and intimacy all its own—a sense of seclusion and enclosure rarely found in a larger yard.

A small garden can take on almost any personality or style. It can be a lush tropical grotto or an English-style cottage garden. It can be a formal little jewel of a knot garden, or a rustic retreat. It can even offer a cornucopia of edibles—beds of vegetables, and fruit tree gracefully espaliered against a sunny wall.

The secret to creating a wonderful small-space garden lies in the artful combination of the practical with the esthetic. In this book you'll find plenty of help in both areas. To start off, you'll learn the tricks landscape designers use to make the most of a little space. You'll see how to use design principles such as scale, balance, unity, variety, and accent to plan your garden. Then, for an inspiring look at the results you can achieve using these principles, turn to the photo gallery, where you'll see delightful gardens in a dazzling array of styles. Finally, you'll find practical help in the form of a catalog of some of the best small-space plants, plus solid advice on planting and caring for the plants you choose.

So dream, plan, and enjoy— you're well on your way to transforming *your* little plot of land into the garden of your dreams!

For their help in preparing this book, special thanks go to Rebecca La Brum for carefully editing the manuscript and to JoAnn Masaoka Van Atta for styling some of the photographs.

Photographers: **Douglas Bond:** 53 bottom; **Glenn Christiansen:** 17, 71 top, 75 bottom; **Peter Christiansen:** 53 top, 75 top; **Claire Curran:** 47 right; **Harry Haralambau:** 10; **Phil Harvey:** 4, 14; **Saxon Holt:** 1, 2, 7 bottom left and right, 11 left, 20, 22 right, 36, 38 top, 39, 41, 46 bottom, 64 bottom, 68 bottom; **Horticultural Photography:** 28 left; **Michael Landis:** 49 bottom; **Steve Marley:** 29 right, 59 bottom; **Ells Marugg:** 44; **Jack McDowell:** 19; **Michael McKinley:** 28 right; **Richard Nicol:** 6, 7 top, 42 bottom, 61 top, 73 top, 76; **Don Normark:** 22 center, 26, 59 top, 62, 65, 72; **Norman Plate:** 23 center, 24, 38 bottom, 43, 46 top, 47 left, 49 top, 54, 58 bottom, 60, 61 bottom, 64 top, 70, 73 bottom; **Bill Ross:** 8, 28 center, 29 center, 40 top, 42 top, 48, 52 bottom; **David Stubbs:** 25; **K. Bryan Swezey:** 92; **Michael Thompson:** 34, 52 top, 55 bottom, 67, 69, 94; **Verna Van de Water:** 66; **Darrow Watt:** 11 right, 23 right, 40 bottom, 50, 55 top, 57, 74, 89; **Peter Whiteley:** 45, 58 top, 63; **Doug Wilson:** 71 bottom; **Tom Wyatt:** 12, 22 left, 23 left, 29 left, 51, 68 top.

Cover: Flowing lines of brick paving and gently mounded planting beds visually enlarge this tranquil garden. For another view, see page 1. Landscape designer: Konrad Gauder/ Landsculpture. Cover design by Susan Bryant. Photography by Saxon Holt.

Contents

Special Features

*A gravel path curves out of sight, creating an illusion
of distance. Plants use every available growing space, twining
upward and blooming from containers. A simple color scheme
unifies the landscape. Design: Josephine Zeitlin.*

The Small-Space Garden

By choice or by circumstance, more and more of us today have small gardens. In many parts of the country, the rising value of land has meant a decided decrease in the size of housing units and lots—and gardens. And for the ever-increasing segment of the population living in cities, the intimate urban patio or pocket-size yard has replaced broad, rolling lawns and spacious flower beds as the norm.

Of course, "small" is a relative term that means different things to different people. To some, "small" describes the length of a patio, deck, or doorstep, to others a backyard complete with a pool and swaying palms. Even large properties share the attributes of small gardens if usable space is divided into small or odd-shaped parcels—or if the owners simply want to achieve the intimacy that a little garden can offer.

Regardless of the precise size of *your* small garden, you'll use the same design principles to make the most of its space. And you'll find that while a small garden undeniably presents challenges both practical and esthetic, it needn't limit you either in the style of garden you create or in the type of gardening you do.

Every Detail Counts

Small-space gardening anywhere brings special problems and unique rewards. If the fuchsias faint, a shrub turns shabby, or a brick lies askew, you'll notice right away, since nothing is far from view. But by the same token, just one or two vibrant specimens in a small space can have more impact than masses of the same plant in a larger landscape. Seen at close range, a single flowering tree can be studied and fully appreciated in every detail—for its color, texture, form, and fragrance. Likewise, a simple path or stone bench is more likely to give delight in the context of a small space than it would in a more expansive setting.

A small garden has other advantages, too. It can have a soothing, sheltered intimacy that larger yards lack. And its modest maintenance requirements can seem more a carefree pleasure than an overwhelming responsibility: you can dig, thin, weed, prune, mow, clip, harvest, sweep, water, and fertilize in a fraction of the time a big yard would require. Of course, limited space doesn't mean you have to forego the pleasures of serious gardening; if you enjoy hoeing, mowing, raking, and generally puttering outdoors, you can design a garden to satisfy your tastes.

A Quick Tour of this Book

Whether you're starting from scratch or simply relandscaping, you'll have to put in some work to create the pleasant, relaxing garden of your dreams. Let this book serve as a partner in your endeavors, whatever their scope and scale. Each chapter offers guidelines to help you visualize, design, and finally implement your garden plan.

The following chapter, "Planning the Small Garden," lays down the basics for a thoughtfully designed project. You'll learn how to take advantage of every inch of available space, and you'll discover some landscaping tricks to make your space seem bigger. To demonstrate the variety of approaches that a single small garden can accommodate, we've included design plans for one site as envisioned by landscape architects in four different regions of the United States.

"Making the Most of Your Space" then illustrates these design and problem-solving principles. You'll go on a photographic garden tour to see how the design theories introduced in the previous chapter have been put to use in real gardens.

In the final chapter, "Plant Selection & Care," you'll find tips on choosing small-space plants, plus a short catalog of highly recommended choices— from shrubs that don't outgrow their welcome to colorful, easily trained vines that won't stage a total garden takeover. And you'll find guidelines for planting and caring for the plants you choose.

Cool Harmony

Lush green ground cover contrasts with the gray severity of concrete paving, dividing this seasoned patio into boldly outlined rectangles. Cool, harmonious hues of furnishings and container-grown Lychnis coeli-rosa give a sense of spaciousness. Design: R. David Adams Associates, Inc.

A Pocket of Privacy

Planted and paved, a pocket-size niche outside a bathroom window becomes a cool, leafy garden. Wood trellis adds to the sheltered effect, creating depth and defining a raised bed spilling over with nandina. Concave boulder surrounded by pachysandra catches rain water. Southern magnolia tree softens far wall. Design: John M. Bernhard.

Vantage Point

A distant view of rolling hills extends the borders of this colorful deck garden. Small deck steps down in two levels, making the space seem larger, and the open design of the fence adds to the illusion. Built-in corner planter is also a space-saver. Pots brim with plants in bright but cool colors, among them phlox, clarkia, and alstroemeria. A sliding glass door provides a graceful transition between indoors and out, mirroring the deck's plants and revealing foliage from a pot-grown tree inside.

*A straight line is the shortest distance between two points, but
strong curves make the space seem greater. Ground cover
between bold pavers defines the curves; a profusion of bloom
crowds up to brick path. Design: Katzmaier Newell Kehr.*

Planning
—
the Small
—
Garden

A successful garden of any size is rarely the result of chance: it is almost always the product of careful planning. For the small-space gardener, the planning process is doubly important. Every element of the garden is seen close up, and every detail has impact.

There are probably as many ways to transform a small space into a satisfying garden as there are people approaching the task. As evidenced by the four different interpretations shown on pages 30–33, there's no single ideal approach to any particular site—the plan that's right for you must suit your own needs and personality.

Begin by making a conscious effort to think spatially. Try viewing the space as an outdoor room with a floor, walls, and a ceiling, all of which can be decorated, just as the elements of an indoor room can.

Use this book as a guide, but don't make it your sole resource. It's important to get out and see how design principles are interpreted in real gardens and how plants actually behave. Find out if garden clubs offer tours of interesting local gardens. Look around your neighborhood, go to landscape shows, visit display gardens at local nurseries.

It's also a good idea to keep an idea file. Comb magazines and books for pictures of pleasing landscapes, flower beds, decks, fences, specimen plants—anything and everything that appeals to you. Take photos of gardens you like. It's all grist for the mill when planning time comes.

Defining Your Needs

What do you want from your garden? Your aim may be to create a private, restful retreat, a place to entertain, a children's play area, or a source of cut flowers or vegetables. You may have one or several goals. When space is limited, though, you must rank these goals according to importance, then concentrate on those at the top of the list.

Many people automatically make a lawn their first priority simply because they associate a carpet of grass with the idea of a garden. But unless you have a real need for grass as a soft play surface, think twice before devoting valuable space to a lawn.

Once you've listed your needs, decide on the desired level of maintenance. Do you enjoy spending your leisure time keeping your garden looking its best? Or do you prefer a garden that demands minimal care? Keep in mind that a small garden must be presentable: every weed, every wayward branch is more conspicuous than it would be in a larger space. Also be aware that certain elements require more upkeep than others. The following list ranks common garden elements in order of maintenance demands, from the *least* care for structures and paving to the *most* (usually) for flowers.

- Structures and paving
- Trees and large shrubs
- Shrub borders and screens
- Ground covers
- Lawn
- Perennial and annual flowers

One-note Harmony

Limited space doesn't mean you can't opt for a formally laid-out garden. Here, a single rose variety is set out in precise symmetry around a garden focal point.

Style Setters

Garden style is more a matter of taste than space, as evidenced by serene Japanese-influenced garden at left (Design: Maz Imazuni) and glorious potpourri of bloom at right.

Your choice of specific plant categories will also influence how much care is required; see pages 27–28 and 78–87 for more on plant selection.

Choosing a Garden Style

If your garden is small, it's crucial to choose a single style you can live with comfortably. There's no room for a confusion of styles, and there's no escaping from day to day the theme you've selected. Still, you needn't let limited space drastically restrict your choices; in even the smallest area, it's possible to suggest a style. For example, just a tiny pocket of ground planted with a leafy surround and blanketed with ferns is enough to suggest a woodland garden. A small space can also provide a perfect setting for a riotous cottage garden, a neatly structured knot garden, a tropical garden, and so on.

Many themes can be interpreted either formally or informally, depending on your taste. An informal garden is characterized by a lack of symmetry and by flowing lines, curves, and natural-looking plant forms; a formal one, on the other hand, is typically symmetrical, featuring straight or geometric lines and plants trained or clipped into unnatural forms (sheared hedges and topiary, for example). A water garden with a rectangular pool flanked by two identical square planting beds is distinctly formal, but if it had an irregularly shaped pond in a woodland setting, such a garden would be informal.

Some styles wouldn't look right if designed formally. A rustic garden requires an informal appearance; the same is true of a cottage garden, which should at least *look* unplanned and untamed.

The garden style you choose should be compatible with the area where you live, the architecture of your house, and the interior from which you view the garden. If your architecture or the decor of the room opening onto the garden is formal and your taste in landscaping is informal, you may want to temper the garden's natural look with a few formal touches. Repeating an architectural or decor feature outdoors can help tie house and garden together.

Assessing Your Site

Making a detailed sketch of the garden site is an essential part of the planning process—it helps you get organized, gives you a sense of order, and encourages you to think through every step.

Measure the site with a 50- or 100-foot tape measure for precise positioning of features. As you measure, make a rough diagram, recording all dimensions. Note which direction is north, and indicate all the features that will influence your plan: structures, means of access to the garden, any existing plants you want to save, sunny and shady areas, wind directions (to identify windbreak needs), slopes and other changes in elevation, power lines and other utilities, hose bibs, and any irrigation lines. Indicate both desirable and undesirable views. If existing plants are growing poorly, have your soil analyzed (check the Yellow Pages under Laboratories—Testing).

After making your rough sketch, neatly redraw the diagram to scale on graph paper. The most common scale for small-space garden design is 1 inch to either 2 or 4 feet of actual space, but you can use any convenient ratio. An architect's scale—a triangular ruler that converts measurements into different ratios—makes the job easier. Such scales are sold in many art supply stores. A circle template and a landscape template may also be useful.

Before attempting to plan the space you've drawn, review the following discussion of design techniques and garden elements. Think about how they were used in the best small gardens you've seen. Once you have a basic understanding of what is involved, you can begin to develop your design in earnest.

Principles of Design

The same general guidelines apply to the design of all gardens, large or small. Here, though, we have focused on applying these principles to create a successful small garden.

Unity

Unity is that intangible quality that joins all parts of the garden into a pleasing whole. When a small garden is unified, it feels comfortable and gives the illusion of more space.

To achieve unity in your garden, choose a style and stick to it (see page 11). If you don't have a theme at all, you'll find it difficult to connect the elements of the garden. At the other extreme, if you mix a number of styles, you'll end up with a discordant hodgepodge.

Repeating garden elements helps tie everything together. For example, use the same type of brick or stonework throughout the garden, or repeat the same plants in different places. Repetition of colors can also unify a garden; white and gray have well-deserved reputations in this regard.

Finally, designing the entire space at once—even if you don't do all the work at the same time—is more likely to give you a harmonious end result than if you do it piecemeal.

Simplicity

Generally speaking, the smaller the garden, the simpler it should be. Eliminate unnecessary details. If an element doesn't contribute significantly to the composition, don't include it.

Repetition of elements, already mentioned as a means of achieving unity, can also help simplify a small garden; you might use more of the same type of plant rather than introduce new kinds, for example.

Variety

Not even the smallest garden should be so simple that it is monotonous. The trick is to add variety without mixing up too many styles or making the space seem cluttered. Think of quality rather than quantity: instead of using a greater assortment of plants or structures, look for a few elements that can

Small World

Rich in details, miniaturized landscape fills a shady niche against house with lush plantings. Design: Josephine Zeitlin.

bring interest to the garden without complicating it. Container plants accomplish this task well; the pots can be replanted seasonally and displayed in different areas at different times of the year. You might also use an unusual construction material, or put in plants with something "extra"—perhaps fragrance, colorful fruit, or an attractive branching habit.

Accent

A structure such as a gazebo, a special feature like a pond, a piece of statuary, a particularly handsome specimen plant—these are all examples of garden accents or focal points. A focal point attracts and holds the eye and keeps it from seeing the entire garden immediately. A small garden should have at least one major focal point, though there can be several lesser accents as well.

An accent also directs the viewer's gaze away from areas you'd rather not emphasize. If there are unattractive views that can't be completely masked, position the accent in another part of the garden to focus attention on a more pleasing sight.

Balance

To create a balanced garden, you need simply distribute the total visual weight equally around the major accent or focal point. This doesn't mean the

Designing Your Landscape

Planning a garden is one of the most creative home projects you can undertake. Whether you call in a landscaping professional or not, your garden should reflect *your* dreams and needs, *your* likes and dislikes, and *your* notion of what a garden should be.

Long before you even begin to formulate a plan, you'll want to create a file of garden ideas. And even if you do eventually enlist professional help, it's useful to learn as much as you can about landscaping: read gardening books, visit arboretums, even take a class in landscape design.

When the time comes to decide between hiring a professional or designing the garden yourself, several factors will influence your decision. The most important question to ask is this: do you really want to do it yourself? Unless budget is the sole consideration, it won't be worth the effort if it isn't any fun.

Next, consider the scale and complexity of the project and the extent of your knowledge. If you're faced with creating an all-new landscape on a completely blank site, if your site presents complications such as chronic drainage problems, steep hills, or an unusual lot shape, or if major construction is required, you may want to consult a professional. But redesigning an already existing small garden, adding a new element such as a deck, and reworking planting beds are rewarding projects you can probably complete on your own.

If you design it yourself... To design the way professionals do, begin with a careful analysis of what you already have, what you want to save, and what you want to remove or screen from view. On graph paper, draw a detailed base plan showing all the existing elements (see page 11). Be as accurate and detailed as possible, since your future design calculations will be based on this "map."

List all the landscape components you and your family consider most important—perhaps a children's play area, a vegetable garden, and a built-in barbecue area. Don't forget the strictly utilitarian elements, such as a place for refuse cans or a dog run.

Then start experimenting. Sketch various plans on tracing paper taped over your base plan, positioning decks, walkways, pools, flower beds, trees, and so on. Keep an open mind and play with shapes: for example, try one plan with gently curving flower beds, another with geometric forms. Try elevation changes, such as raised beds or low, rolling mounds.

To help visualize a design, you can outline decks, planting beds, and other elements on the ground with stakes and powdered gypsum (or even flour). If the size or shape doesn't look right, simply "erase" the gypsum with water and try again.

Once you've settled on your final design, draw up the plan accurately and to scale. Now you can select plants, choose materials and designs for structural elements such as pathways and decks, and add provisions for irrigation. When the plan is complete, you can implement it yourself or call in a landscape contractor. Call your city building department to find out about permits needed for fences, decks, and pools; also check for easements.

If you decide on a professional... If designing a landscape doesn't appeal to you, or if the project is too complex, you can contact a variety of professionals for assistance. A *landscape architect* holds a university degree in landscape architecture and/or a license certifying completion of the Uniform National Examination in Landscape Architecture (many states *require* this license). These professionals can provide a range of services, from hourly consultation to preparation of complete design and construction drawings. Many belong to the American Society of Landscape Architects (ASLA).

Landscape designers can prepare overall garden design and planting plans, but they aren't licensed. Their training and experience vary; some are graduates of horticulture or garden design programs in 2- or 4-year colleges, while others have the same training as landscape architects. Where state laws limit their work to nonstructural design, they sometimes work through a licensed contractor, architect, or engineer.

Landscape contractors are trained to install paving, structures, lighting, and irrigation systems. They implement the landscape plans; many will design the projects they build.

Nursery personnel are sometimes available for design consultation, and there may be a staff designer who can prepare plans using the nursery's plants and accessories. Some nurseries even have complete design and construction services.

Word-of-mouth is usually the best advertisement for a good landscaping professional of any type. Seek recommendations from friends and neighbors, or from architects or builders. If you lack a personal referral, ask at your local nursery, call the local chapter of the ASLA for a list of members, or consult the Yellow Pages. Ask a prospective designer for a list of previous clients, then look at finished gardens and talk with owners.

garden design must be symmetrical to be balanced. Rather, the sum of interest on one side of the focal point should equal the sum of interest on the other. Don't concentrate the visual weight along one wall or in one corner; in a small space, this sort of imbalance is especially noticeable.

After your plan is on paper, test it for balance by drawing a line through the accent from where you are most likely to stand when you view the garden, usually the house or patio. The two sections don't have to be the same size or contain the same elements, but each should offer approximately the same amount of visual interest.

Scale

Plants and garden structures should be in proportion to the house, plot, and surroundings. Don't use elements more suited to a grander scale—that's like cramming bulky furniture into a small room. It's just as much of a mistake to make everything small just because the yard is small. If the garden elements are too diminutive, they'll be dominated by the house and surroundings.

Scale is sometimes difficult to measure precisely. You'll know that the scale is right if indoor and outdoor spaces seem to flow into one another comfortably—but how do you plan for that?

Country Charm

Unified structural details and a color scheme limited to a few hues are space-enhancers in this garden retreat, cozy as floral chintz in a country parlor. Moss-edged brick pavers are set in sand. For another view of garden, see page 4. Design: Josephine Zeitlin.

Once again, thinking of your garden space as an outdoor room is helpful. You wouldn't use bulky redwood furniture in a very small garden, just as you wouldn't put a massive couch and overstuffed chairs in a tiny den. A 10- by 12-foot potting shed would be in scale in a large garden, but the same structure would overwhelm a small yard—just as a large dresser would overpower a small bedroom.

Consider mature size when selecting plants, since large-growing specimens can take over the entire garden space. A deodar cedar (*Cedrus deodara*) looks innocent enough in its nursery can, but it can grow rapidly, eventually reaching 80 feet tall with a 40-foot spread at the base.

Color in a Small Space

The use of color in a small garden is critical: it can open up the space or make it seem more confined. The most important factor in determining this is whether plant colors are warm or cool.

On the color wheel (shown at right), cool colors are grouped on one side, warm colors on the other. Cool colors—those centered on green, blue, and violet—tend to retreat visually, giving the impression of greater space. Warm colors—those clustered around yellow, orange, and red—seem to surge forward, making the space look smaller.

Cool colors are usually most effective in a small garden, but you don't have to limit yourself to them. You may want to use contrasting colors—for example, violet and yellow or any two other colors directly opposite each other on the color wheel. If you use warm and cool colors together, keep in mind that it takes about four or five times as much of the cool color to balance the warm. This is because warm colors jump out and demand attention—the characteristic that makes them good accents.

Though it's possible to mix many colors in a small garden, it's usually harder to do so successfully than in a larger area. Unless you have a special feeling for color, it's advisable to stick with a few colors, including a dominant one. (Cottage gardens are obvious exceptions; they're meant to display a riot of color.)

Because flower color is easily provided, many gardeners are tempted to build the garden around it. But this color is usually transitory, so it is in fact a poor foundation. Even in a traditional cottage garden, which seems to contain nothing but flowers, there is a framework—often a brick or stone wall or yew hedge. It's best to build the main structure of your garden with trees and shrubs that provide green color over a long season. And you'll find that a leafy green background gives other colors in the garden maximum impact.

Color Wheel

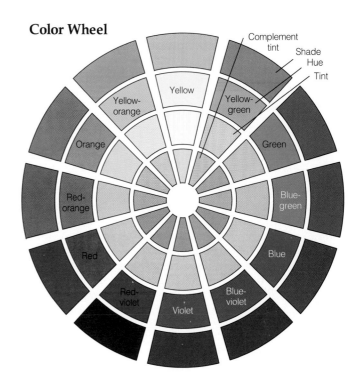

To make your garden inviting and attractive throughout the year, plan for a progression of color. Flowers, fruit, leaves, and even bark can all provide a colorful show in certain seasons. Don't forget about structural and paving materials, outdoor furniture, containers, and other objects in the garden. You won't achieve the desired effect if the colors of structural and other materials don't mesh.

Making a Garden Seem Larger

A small space needn't seem confined. Even a tiny garden can be made to appear more expansive through the use of certain landscaping techniques and optical illusions.

Disguising the Boundaries

A small space looks more restricted when its boundaries are obvious. If fences or walls clearly define your yard, you can obscure them with trees, shrubs, or vines—masses of greenery that will blur the sharp distinction between your garden and the neighboring property.

Even if a boundary is visible, you can call it into question by implying that more lies beyond. For example, you might construct a pathway that disappears around a bend near the edge of the garden. Though the path may actually end just out of sight behind shrubbery, it still seems to lead to another part of the garden that can't immediately be seen. A door in a high wall or fence, especially one at the back of the garden, serves the same purpose. The door doesn't have to open or lead anywhere—in fact, it can even be a painting. Real or not, it's an effective focal point, drawing the eye to the fringe of the yard and giving the impression that there's more to be seen beyond the fence.

Borrowing Scenery

To expand the borders of your garden visually, try the Japanese technique of borrowing scenery: incorporate attractive plantings or structures next door—or in the distance—into your plan. If your neighbor has a large tree, plant smaller trees in front of it so that the entire planting appears to belong to your garden. If there's a mass of handsome shrubbery near your property, include it in your design. Even a distant vista, such as a rolling hillside or a grove of stately trees, can be framed from your garden.

Concealing & Revealing

Instilling a garden with a sense of mystery and anticipation makes the space seem bigger. The Japanese developed a technique to accomplish this centuries ago: they concealed parts of the garden from initial view, then gradually revealed them. For example, shrubs might screen part of a view—perhaps an arbor or a distant panorama—from the house or patio. Only beyond the shrub screen is the entire view revealed. This technique makes it impossible to judge the extent of a space at first glance.

Lines That Curve

Uninterrupted straight lines often lead the eye too quickly to the periphery of the garden, making the space seem smaller. But curved or rounded lines add a meandering, expansive quality; even a bend in an otherwise straight path slows down the eye and diverts attention from the garden's boundary.

Curved lines in your garden should be sweeping, never tentative or merely wiggly. Follow the example of professional landscape designers and use C- or S-shaped curves to form paths, beds, and other garden elements; such curves make bold and forceful design statements.

Cool Colors & Fine Textures

Because they seem to retreat into the background, cool colors help create the illusion of greater space (see "Color in a Small Space," facing page). Fine textures, too, can make a plant (page 27) or structure appear to recede. For example, choose narrow fence boards rather than wide ones; for pavement, use brick or cobbles instead of large flagstones.

Creating Depth

If a small garden looks deep—if it seems to extend well away from the house—it feels more spacious. To give your garden a feeling of depth, start by providing a route through it. A garden that can't be strolled through and viewed from different angles looks flat and two-dimensional. You can also add depth by arranging plants in certain ways. For example, at the outer edges of the garden, mass vines, small trees, and shrubs of different shapes, heights, textures, and shades of green. Such an irregular border produces a greater sensation of depth than does a solid, unadorned fence or uniform hedge.

Double-planting at the periphery—placing one row of plants in front of another—is also effective; the greenery appears to go back farther than it really does. There's room for double-planting in most small gardens if you choose plants of suitable size and growth habit.

You'll emphasize the feeling of depth by placing light-colored or variegated plants in front of darker green ones. Or position airy shrubs or small trees in front of denser plants, so that you see the background only through a lacy foliage screen. Instead of just covering a wall with vines, add dimension by planting a few tall shrubs in front of it as well.

Structures can be "layered" for greater depth, too. You might affix a trellis (with or without a plant trained on it) to a vertical surface, or decorate a tall brick or concrete wall with attached planters, a wall fountain, a plaque, or other ornament.

When sculpting mounds (see "Changing Levels," below), create depth by forming a cluster of mounds instead of just one, and by overlapping the mounds.

Exaggerating the difference between close-up and far-off objects creates a powerful sensation of depth. To achieve this sort of exaggeration, combine an advancing foreground with a receding background. Use a small amount of warm color and coarse texture in the foreground, a mass of cool color and fine texture in the background. You'll need about 80 percent cool color to balance 20 percent warm color, and approximately the same ratio of fine to coarse texture. Tip the scales and you'll lose the feeling of depth.

Changing Levels

Level changes give the illusion of greater space by offering a different perspective from various parts of the garden. The change need not be drastic; if emphasized by steps or planting beds, even a drop of a few inches can be effective.

For a horizontal change of levels, you can form mounds and swales (dips). All you have to do is move soil from one place to another. And if you mound the same amount that you excavate, you

(Continued on page 21)

Tropical Hideaway

Lush foliage in the ground and in containers makes a tropical retreat of an area just 15 feet wide. Swirls of brick paving set on sand lead to raised 9- by 12-foot pool; bricks were split to fit pattern. Design: Robbie Wallace.

Rising above the Ordinary

Design puzzle: Your front yard is on a slight incline, and you'd like something more interesting than a plain slope of lawn leading to the front door. *Grower's dilemma:* You want to fit a vegetable patch into the design of your small garden. *Traffic problem:* Your plans call for plenty of casual garden seating and a flower bed, but space is tight. *The solution?* In all three cases, the dilemma can be resolved simply by building a raised bed.

A series of raised beds provides a gently sloping site with a graceful transition from one level to another. And raised beds are perfect for growing vegetables; the sun-warmed, well-drained soil can produce bumper crops early in the season. Finally, a raised bed built with a wide top cap provides space for flowers, extra seating, *and* a comfortable place for the gardener to rest while weeding and pruning.

From a design point of view, raised beds offer several advantages. They use space efficiently and create smooth transitions from one ground level to the next. And through their strong structural statement, they help unify various garden elements, particularly if you're careful to build them from materials that harmonize with the surroundings.

From a gardener's point of view, a raised bed allows you to grow plants that otherwise might not favor your garden, since you can control soil composition and drainage. Raised beds are excellent for elevating vegetables and flowers to a convenient working level and for displaying all plants impressively, whether you want to showcase a specialty plant or just bring small specimens closer to eye level.

Design and materials. Raised beds fall into two general categories: box-type beds and low, stepped beds that are really like miniature retaining walls. Within these two basic types, wide variations are possible; you can adjust the design and materials to get just what you want.

Box-type beds can be almost any size — from 3 to 10 feet long (or longer), from less than a foot to over 3 feet tall. They can be made from almost any material you'd use for a wall: brick, stone, concrete, or wood (decay-resistant redwood, cedar, or cypress, or pressure-treated lumber, at least 2 inches thick for sturdiest beds). *Note:* Since pressure-treated wood is impregnated with a pesticide, some experts suggest that you plant food crops at least a foot away, root crops at least 2 feet from the treated wood.

For a finished look, you can stain plank boxes and add detailing to tie the beds into the overall landscape design. To fit into a more rustic landscape, box-type beds can be built of railroad ties, pressure-treated landscape 4-by timbers, or logs (whole or cut in half). Beds made from vertical wood stakes placed close together in a row are another option; these can look rustic or sophisticated, depending on how they're finished.

One unusual and space-efficient way to use wooden box beds is to stack them as shown at left. The three cedar frames placed atop one another in alternating diamond fashion make a unique "ziggurat-style" box garden that can hold 20 or more different kinds of vegetables or flowers. Amazingly, the entire asssembly fits into a space just 4 feet square.

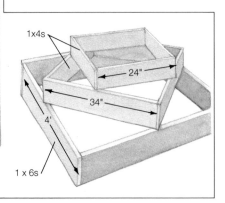

Formed by stacking three cedar boxes, this "ziggurat-style" bed boasts a lush planting of 20 different crops; a trellis adds vertical growing space.

Most simple raised beds that can be built of wood can also be constructed of masonry—brick, stone, or concrete (poured concrete or broken pieces from former pavings). This means you can plan raised beds to fit in with the materials used in your overall design.

Both masonry and wood are appropriate materials for low, stepped beds that make the transition up gradual slopes. Each change in level can be quite small (the height of a single railroad tie or landscape timber) or a little deeper (the width of a 2 by 12 plank).

Technical tips. A raised bed is somewhat like a low retaining wall (see pages 44–45), but with one significant difference: it rarely has to withstand the soil pressure exerted on most retaining walls. For this reason, building a sturdy raised bed is not difficult. Under some conditions, however, raised beds may be subject to the same restrictions that apply to retaining walls; if your bed will be higher than 3 feet, or if you're planning to build it on sloping or unstable ground, check with your local building department before starting construction.

Drainage is important in any kind of raised bed. If the bed is open to the ground at the bottom, most excess water will drain out. (You should turn hard soil below the box with a spade for better drainage.) A closed-bottom box should have weep holes drilled in the sides a few inches up from the ground, spaced 2 to 3 feet apart. It's also a good idea to place at least a 4-inch layer of crushed rock in a closed bed before you add soil.

A simple plank raised bed can be made by nailing side boards to 4 by 4 corner posts, then setting the bottomless box over predug post holes and packing soil in around posts. Make

Distinctive textured brick bed elevates the status of an Indian laurel fig tree and increases landscape interest by adding a new garden level. Double corner at right keeps planter from projecting too far out at house corner. Design: The Peridian Group.

corner posts long enough to extend into the soil below the side boards a foot or more. (Posts don't *have* to be sunk into the ground, but the bed will be more secure if they are.) If you build a bed longer than 12 feet, nail side boards to posts sunk midway along the inside edges of the long side to prevent bowing. If moles or gophers are a problem, you can line the bottom of the bed with wire screening.

Railroad ties or landscape timbers may be stacked, then anchored with steel pipes or rods driven down through the corners a foot or more into the ground (drill holes for the pipes before driving them through). You can build a low vertical wood stake bed by driving 2 by 2 stakes side by side into the ground or by embed-

ding them in a small poured concrete footing.

Masonry beds are built in the same way as walls of the same materials; they require trenching and footings (usually concrete).

The best soil mix to use in your raised bed depends on what you're planting; check individual plant requirements. If the beds are open at the bottom, you can remove dense earth below the box and replace it with amended soil to improve growing conditions further. Be sure to tamp a ledge of earth around the inside to support the box.

Before planting, soak the soil so it settles to a natural level. Be sure to keep the soil surface about 1 to 2 inches below the top of the bed.

Up, Down & Around

Curving lines and changes in level make this graceful garden seem larger. The S curve of the deck draws the eye to the pool shown in photo at right (left side of garden, above). The pool's fountain and its backdrop of redwoods hide neighboring house. Trellis on garage walls, draped with grape vines, adds dimension and growing space. A dove tree (Davidia involucrata) tops the C-shaped mound at right, above. Design: Judith L. Donaghey.

. . . Continued from page 16

won't have to purchase additional soil—or haul the excess away.

A note of caution about sculpting the earth: the object is to create gentle swells and hollows, not abrupt peaks and valleys. Mounds and swales must look like natural contours if they are to be effective, and they must be in scale with the garden. Be critical. Stand back and ask yourself whether the contour you've created looks like an unplanned part of the landscape. If it doesn't, reshape it until you're satisfied with the result.

Building raised beds is another relatively easy way to change levels (see pages 18–19 for details). To underscore the effect, make the beds different heights. Constructing a terrace, patio, or deck either higher or lower than the surrounding terrain also adds dimension, though this is clearly a greater undertaking than putting together a raised bed.

To change levels at the garden skyline, use structures such as trellises, fences, walls, pergolas, and arbors. These are also invaluable in creating walls and ceilings for privacy (see below).

Other Illusions

A strategically placed mirror will reflect plants and structures, producing an image that looks like an extension of the garden. A well-executed mural is another good illusion; painted on a high wall or fence, it can make the space seem larger by providing an image that's engrossing to view. Garden boundaries will recede even farther if the background is painted so that it appears to dwindle into the distance.

Try another trick of perspective: gradually narrow a path as it leads toward the edge of the garden. The perimeter will seem farther off than it really is.

Using dwarf or smaller-growing varieties of plants usually seen in much larger forms can be a very effective illusion; the eye is tricked into thinking the scale is bigger than it really is, making the rest of the garden look more spacious by comparison. For good plant choices, consult the guide on pages 78–87 and check with nurseries for small-growing varieties available locally. An alternative to growing dwarf varieties is to pot larger-growing plants in containers; you'll effectively limit their growth by restricting root space.

A Sense of Privacy

Walls and ceilings fulfill the same function in a garden as they do in a house: they provide privacy. A wall can be an actual structure (such as a fence) or a screen of shrubs or trees. Structures offer immediate privacy, but by themselves they can be stark and imposing. Plants have a softer look but can take years to reach screening size. To get the best of both

worlds—instant privacy and good looks—try using structures and plants in combination. Cloaked or partially screened with greenery, a fence or wall won't look as stark; the plants help lend a feeling of depth, too.

Ceilings can consist of structures such as patio roofs, overhangs, arbors, and pergolas; if grown with vines, they'll look softer and offer even more privacy. Tree canopies high enough to walk under also make effective ceilings. Positioned near garden boundaries, these "ceilings" can double as walls.

Though trees are useful for masking undesirable views, large plants aren't always necessary for privacy. Shrubs or vines that extend above eye level will screen you from neighbors in the adjacent yard; chest-high plants provide privacy when you are sitting.

Structures should reach at least slightly higher than eye level to give seclusion. Check with your local building department for restrictions on height and location of fences, walls, and other structures.

Space Savers

To make the maximum use of your limited space, incorporate some of the following features and techniques into your plan.

Vertical Gardening

Vining plants are indispensable in a small garden: they grow upward, thus saving valuable ground space. If trained on walls or other structures near the edges of the garden, climbing plants help give privacy; when trained over an arbor or pergola, they form ceilings and provide shade. They're also effective in softening hard lines in the landscape and disguising unsightly structures and utility areas. A vine-covered trellis, for example, does a beautiful job of hiding garbage cans, stacked firewood, or bags of potting soil.

Vining vegetables such as pole beans, squash, and cucumbers can be trained upward on trellises and wire fences. Grown this way, they're also easier to tend and to harvest (see page 75).

Some woody plants with pliable stems, such as pyracantha and apple, can be espaliered—trained to grow flat against a vertical surface (see pages 56–57). Espaliering saves space and adds dimension to walls at the same time.

Small Planting Beds

Save space in a small garden by scaling down planting beds. A diminutive border or raised bed spilling over with annuals and perennials easily catches the eye. A large container crowded with enough different annuals to make a bouquet can even take the place of a planting bed (see pages 66–67). Small raised beds filled with improved soil make an ideal small-space vegetable garden.

Built-ins

Make more efficient use of your space with built-in furniture and storage areas. You can build benches onto a deck or circling a tree, making sure that their dimensions are in keeping with the small scale of the garden. For even greater efficiency, conceal storage space under lift-up lids.

Another good option is a snug lean-to shed built against the house or garage or onto a sturdy fence or garden wall. Make the shed unobtrusive by using materials that blend with the main structure.

Access to the Garden

If you don't have an easy route into the garden, you'll seldom use it; the situation is worse if you can't even view the garden from indoors. A garden that you can see and walk into easily will become an integral part of your living space.

The best access is one that merges house and garden, expanding both indoor and outdoor spaces by treating the garden as an outdoor room attached to the house. Developed to its full potential in California, this style of landscaping is applicable anywhere, even in cold climates—if the garden isn't always an agreeable place to be, at least with good access it can always provide a welcoming view.

There are many ways to make indoor and outdoor spaces flow together. If you don't have a satisfactory view of the garden, consider installing a window; sliding glass or French doors also make it easier to get to the garden. Improving access may also mean widening a doorway or adding a deck, terrace, or stairway.

Continuity of style helps merge house and garden; you might lay down similar flooring material in adjoining indoor and outdoor spaces or use the same color scheme or furniture style. Indoor plants in the room opening onto the garden also create a good bridge to the outdoors.

Structural Elements

A garden is far more than plantings alone, and the way you incorporate structural elements into your design will have a great deal to do with its success.

Seating Areas

As you concentrate on the main seating area—a terrace, deck, or patio—don't overlook the charm that

Optical Illusions

A trio of garden illusions shows how space can be made to seem greater. Jog in path, left, keeps eye from immediately taking in property boundaries (Design: Kenneth Pedersen). Mirror panel, center, seems to double size of shallow pool and patio. At right, painted gate mural implies depth.

minor seating areas can contribute to the garden. Even in a small space, there's usually room for such secondary seating as a wrought-iron bench, a wooden cap on a raised bed, or a natural feature like a large tree stump or flat rock.

While minor seating can be located anywhere, the terrace, deck, or patio is best placed adjacent to the house. It doesn't have to be in the backyard, though; there may be a suitable spot out front or on the side that can be screened from neighbors and street traffic.

When choosing locations for a seating area, consider the exposure, keeping in mind that it's easier to cool down a hot, sunny exposure than to warm up a cool, shady one. The south side of the house, in the path of the sun for most of the day, is warmest, the west side (which gets afternoon sun) is next warmest, followed by the east side, which receives morning sun. The north side is the coldest exposure, since it's shaded almost all day.

Depending on your climate, you may want a completely shaded seating area or one that is sunny at a certain time of day. Observe the sun patterns in your garden and plan accordingly, remembering that in summer the sun rises farther to the east and sets farther to the west than it does in winter. Shadows are shorter during the hot summer months.

In a very hot climate, the north side of the house is a good place to build a deck or patio. If you don't have that option, plan for a shade tree or an overhang, trellis, or other structure over the seating area. If the northern exposure is your only choice in a cooler climate, try to move the seating area away from the house walls; a patio or deck that is perpendicular to the house and juts out into or toward the sunshine may be the answer. To help warm up the area, you can make generous use of inorganic objects like rocks and all manner of pavements, which tend to absorb and hold heat, thus increasing the temperature around them. (In contrast, plants transpire—lose water through evaporation—and cool the air.)

Your deck, terrace, or patio should be only a little larger than you think necessary to accommodate your family and the customary number of guests comfortably; anything bigger than that may be out of scale with the garden. An area measuring 120 square feet (10 feet by 12 feet) is usually adequate for four people, but other sizes and configurations can also work well. For example, a shallow deck or patio that runs the width of the house may encompass a larger area without seeming to occupy a greater part of the garden. To decide on the best size and shape, mark off an area with a garden hose, string, or powdered gypsum and find out if the space feels comfortable. Be sure to take furniture into account; allow room for pulling back chairs and letting people pass by.

Garden Trickery

Path at left hints at hidden spaces, but actually the property ends at a wall a few feet away (Design: Stone & Fischer). In center photo, slight changes in level visually increase yard's depth (Design: John Herbst). At right, a shrub trained as a standard (Lycianthes rantonnei 'Royal Robe') poses as a tree, but the scale is smaller.

Garden Graphics Underfoot

Picture a pathway of square concrete pavers lined up along a narrow side yard, or a small entry patio paved in irregular flagstones. Nice, but nothing special. Now picture the same flagstones outlined in lush dichondra, or the pathway pavers divided by ribbons of ground-hugging plants sprinkled with tiny flowers. The path becomes a clearly defined "dotted line"; the flagstones are now reminiscent of a giraffe's markings!

Planted pavings pack graphic punch that livens up an entire space and gives it a focus. They are perfect accents for small areas: limiting them to a single walkway or pocket-size patio actually adds to their visual impact. Surrounding greenery adds color and texture to stone and masonry surfaces, helping to soften the hard edges. And the miniature quality of the plants can lend a sense of intimacy, inviting you to slow down, look closely, and focus on details. Planted pavings do require more care (watering, weeding, feeding, clipping) than plain ones, but if they're used in small swatches, the effect can outweigh the effort.

Creating a combination of pavings and plantings that is just right for your particular garden allows you to exercise your creativity; it's almost like putting together a quilt or a wood parquet design. You can make a patchwork of squares or diamonds, zigzags, or random, impressionistic shapes. You can contrast colors and textures—perhaps rough-hewn redwood rounds with neat dichondra, or squares of concrete with leafy Indian mock strawberry.

If your overall garden design is on the formal side, consider bold, geometric designs with fine-textured plantings forming strips between pavers or tiles. For a more informal look—the style English gardeners call "crazy paving"—let plantings spill and meander among irregularly shaped stones or broken concrete pieces. Let your imagination and your overall garden "look" guide you.

Paving materials. Types of pavings range from concrete to natural stone to wood. Whatever material you choose, set the pavers in sand or soil rather than mortar, so that plant roots can grow into the soil beneath.

Poured concrete is highly versatile; it can be poured in any shape and finished with a smooth, rough, or pebbled texture. It can be installed in

A flagstone pathway outlined in lush green dichondra lends visual interest to the garden and invites strolling.

a formal or irregular design, with spaces between sections or additional areas left open for planting. *Precast concrete pavers,* relatively inexpensive and widely available, can be laid in a variety of patterns. They come in many shapes; colors range from gray to pale green to brick-pink. *Broken concrete*—irregularly shaped pieces broken up from old concrete paving—is an excellent material for informal walkways; it can be set out to resemble a flagstone pavement.

Brick, either new or salvaged, looks equally handsome in formal or rustic settings, and its texture and warm color contrast nicely with plantings. It's fairly expensive, but easy to work with when laid on sand.

Exterior tile, such as terra cotta, is as easy to lay as brick but considerably costlier. Durable and smooth (it can be slippery when wet), it presents a formal, elegant appearance.

Stone pavings offer the warmth of a thoroughly natural material and are extremely durable. Irregularly-shaped flagstone and slate pieces, though expensive and heavy to handle, make beautiful paths and patios when surrounded by greenery.

Redwood rounds are easy to work with and have a natural, rustic look, but they don't last as long as other materials.

Plant choices. Though no plant stands up to foot traffic as well as stone or masonry, some plants are tougher than others. Those listed here will provide a thick, low carpet of greenery; most bear tiny flowers in spring or summer.

Good choices include ajuga (*Ajuga reptans*); baby's tears (*Soleirolia soleirolii*); Corsican sandwort (*Arenaria balearica*); creeping speedwell (*Veronica repens*); cymbalaria (*Cymbalaria aequitriloba*); dichondra (*Dichondra micrantha*); crane's bill

As soft and colorful as an impressionist's canvas, this garden liberally combines stone, poured-in-place concrete paving, and plants. Moneywort, blue fescue, sweet violet, and succulents fill in pockets with surprising compatibility.

(*Erodium chamaedryoides*); green carpet (*Herniaria glabra*); Indian mock strawberry (*Duchesnea indica*); isotoma or blue star creeper (*Laurentia fluviatilis*); Korean grass (*Zoysia tenuifolia*); lippia (*Phyla nodiflora*); mazus (*Mazus reptans*); moneywort or creeping Jenny (*Lysimachia nummularia*); pratia (*Pratia angulata*); Scotch or Irish moss (*Sagina subulata*); and spring cinquefoil (*Potentilla tabernaemontanii*).

Some suitable ground covers add an extra dimension—fragrance. When crushed underfoot, they exude delightful aromas. Prostrate thymes are among the most reliable fragrant choices; try fuzzy gray-green woolly thyme (*Thymus pseudolanuginosus*) or dark green creeping thyme (*T. serpyllum*), which has lavender flowers in spring. Other possibilities include chamomile (*Chamaemelum nobile*), jewel mint of Corsica (*Mentha*

requienii), and spearmint-smelling yerba buena (*Satureja douglasii*, or the desert form *S. chandleri*).

For further guidelines on choosing any planting, see "Selecting Your Plants," pages 78–87.

Planting and care. If you're dealing with existing pavers, dig out as much of the soil as you can between them to a depth of 3 to 4 inches. Then fill the channels with 1 to 2 inches of rich planting mix, pouring it onto the surface and sweeping it into the cracks with a broom or your hands. For plants that like quick drainage, add sand to the soil. If you are putting down new paving, lay it on firm soil or sand, then fill in the spaces with planting mix.

It's most economical to buy plants in flats; you can also get ground covers in cell-packs and 2-

or 4-inch pots. Cut plants purchased in flats into inch-square plugs, making sure you get a good bit of root with each plug.

To plant, sprinkle the surface with water to settle the soil mix, then let it dry slightly. Space the plugs 4 to 6 inches apart in the channels. With the plants in place, add enough soil mix to reach almost to the level of the pavers. Leave enough room for water to collect in the channels and to keep plant crowns low enough to protect them from foot traffic.

Water the new plants regularly. After they become established, give them a light application of a complete dry or liquid fertilizer. Dry fertilizer can simply be broadcast over the surface, then gently watered in; if using a liquid fertilizer, dilute it according to the manufacturer's directions before applying.

Outdoor Room

Terrace paved with brick and stone is surrounded by 3-foot-high wire fence covered with ivy and fruiting grapes—all that's needed to create privacy for seated diners. Low foliage wall seems to expand space; a higher barrier would have boxed in the small area.

Paving Material

Brick, stone, wood, concrete, quarry tile, slate, gravel—all can be used to cover the surface of pathways, terraces, decks, and patios. Any paving material takes on greater significance in a small garden, so buy good-quality paving and avoid anything too bright or garish; it probably won't look any better in the small space of your garden than it does in the nursery or building center.

Think of ways to add interest to paving. For instance, use a material with an unusual texture, or lay the pieces in an arresting pattern. Combine materials—for example, border brick with wood. If you're using squares of concrete or tile, you might leave some squares in the pavement empty for planting. A small ground cover can also be planted between stones or bricks (see page 24).

Paving can help make the garden seem more spacious. Choose a small, fine paving material rather than a large, coarse one. Lay deck boards horizontally if the garden is very narrow, lengthwise if it's wide and shallow; you can also arrange the boards to direct the eye toward an accent.

Paving can be used to a limited extent to control temperature. Dark surfaces tend to hold heat while light-colored ones reflect heat and are somewhat cooler.

Water Features

Water is a wonderful, magical feature that creates an air of serenity and peace. It shouldn't be precluded simply because of limited space; in fact, a pond, pool, or waterfall can become the central theme of even a very small garden. If you want to conjure up the imagery of water without occupying a great deal of space and without expending much labor and expense, you can do that, too. A small fountain or simple water-spouting pipe set into a wall will serve your purpose.

Lighting

Lighting transforms the garden into a true outdoor room, a place to enjoy—even if only from indoors—at any hour. Unless they're quite decorative, lighting fixtures should be unobtrusive. The light itself should be diffused, bathing the garden in a soft glow; you should never see individual points of bright light. For special effects, position fixtures to uplight, downlight, or backlight plants.

Plants in Your Garden Design

The smaller the space, the more important it is to select plants carefully: the right choices can spell success for the garden. In a small space, each plant is more noticeable, and each has the potential to create an eyesore if it's an inappropriate choice for the location.

When you choose plants, don't consider any one characteristic in isolation; look at the total picture. On pages 78–87, you'll find a discussion of factors such as growth habit, climate, and overall suitability to a small garden, along with specific plant suggestions. Other design-related features are discussed below. Weigh them all carefully.

Plant Form

A plant's form refers to its shape and growth habit—whether it's vining or upright-growing, pyramidal, roundheaded, vase-shaped, sprawling, weeping, spiky, or irregular. A pleasing small-space design features enough different forms to make the garden interesting, but it shouldn't have so much variety that the landscape looks jumbled. (An exception: A closely spaced mass of different forms at the perimeter can be used to create a feeling of depth, as discussed on page 16.)

A rounded shrub like an oleander (Nerium oleander) is a good backdrop for an accent plant with a more unusual shape, such as spiky fortnight lily (Dietes vegeta) or pendulous weeping cherry (Prunus subhirtella 'Pendula'). Weeping plants are also effective in directing attention to a point of interest at ground level, such as a pool.

Use a columnar plant like Irish yew (Taxus baccata 'Stricta') or eugenia (Syzygium paniculatum) to provide height. A pyramidal plant such as dwarf Alberta spruce (Picea glauca 'Conica') makes a good accent among rounded or spreading forms. A small, spreading tree such as silk tree (Albizia julibrissin) gives a feeling of breadth to a small garden.

Don't plant pyramidal or columnar trees or shrubs in locations you know they will outgrow; you won't be able to prune your way out of the resulting problem. These plants have a central leader (one main trunk that grows straight up); if you cut it off, multiple leaders will sprout, changing the form of the plant.

Texture

Texture is an important consideration in selecting plants for a small garden. You can manipulate fine, medium, and coarse textures to make space seem larger; for example, use fine texture in the background and coarse texture close up as an accent (see "Creating Depth," page 16).

Leaf size is the major determinant of a plant's texture. Large-leafed types such as southern magnolia (Magnolia grandiflora), Algerian ivy (Hedera canariensis), and most tropical plants tend to have a coarse appearance. Plants with smaller leaves look finer textured; examples include honey locust (Gleditsia triacanthos), heavenly bamboo (Nandina domestica), and boxwood (Buxus species). A deeply cut or lobed leaf margin also lends a fine-textured look, as in the delicate laceleaf Japanese maple (Acer palmatum 'Dissectum'). If the leaf is very large, though, the foliage will look coarse even if it's lobed; Japanese aralia (Fatsia japonica) is a good example.

Glossiness shifts a plant toward coarse texture, while a dull surface gives it a finer appearance. A glossy surface reflects light, making the leaf shiny and eye-catching; a dull surface absorbs light, so the entire leaf is less noticeable.

Color

Every plant in a small garden should carry its weight by providing color during some part of the year—whether in the form of flowers, fruit, foliage, or bark. Even leaves of a particularly handsome shade of green offer a good contribution.

When planning flower color, think beyond just annuals and perennials. Many trees, shrubs, vines, and ground covers bear showy blossoms. Some of these plants, such as flowering dogwood (Cornus florida), put on a spectacular spring display; others, like bottlebrush (Callistemon), bloom over a long season.

Many plants bring brilliant berries or other fruit to the garden palette. In fall and winter, Arbutus unedo bears the round, red fruit that gives the plant its common name, strawberry tree. Oregon grape (Mahonia aquifolium) produces summer clusters of blue berries that attract birds.

Many deciduous trees and shrubs exhibit colorful foliage in autumn. Fall color is usually more spectacular in cold climates, though some plants—Chinese pistache (Pistacia chinensis), for example—put on a show even in mild-winter areas. Another good mild-winter performer is Chinese tallow tree (Sapium sebiferum), which turns a brilliant neon red if given a sunny location and only a bit of autumn chill. Check with a local nursery for shrubs and trees with reliable fall foliage color in your area.

Some plants have strikingly colored foliage throughout the growing season or even all year long. Flowering plum (Prunus blireiana) is deep purple from spring until leaf fall, as is a purple-leafed variety of Eastern redbud (Cercis canadensis 'Forest Pansy'). Woolly lamb's ears (Stachys byzantina) is grown for its soft, grayish-white foliage, not for its purple summer flowers. Several variegated forms of

Details, Details

Little things mean a lot in a small garden—like a whimsical snail fountain, left; delicate blossoms separating paving stones, center (Design: Katzmaier Newell Kehr); or a decorative space-saving bench incorporated into a fanciful wooden garden wall, right.

evergreen euonymus (*Euonymus japonica*) are sold; some have green leaves with yellow or white edges, others green-rimmed yellow leaves.

Even bark can contribute color to the garden. The bare branches of the redtwig dogwood (*Cornus stolonifera*) are scarlet in winter; the gray or light brown outer bark of crape myrtle (*Lagerstroemia indica*) flakes off to reveal smooth pink inner bark.

Year-round Appeal

In a small garden, where every detail seems to be under a microscope, each plant should look attractive most of the year. This is especially true in temperate areas, where the garden can be used all year.

Choose plants that provide some sort of interest at all times: pleasing shape, attractive branching habit, color, beautiful flower form, fragrance, unusual fruit, and so on. The appeal can be seasonal, as long as the plant doesn't deteriorate into an eyesore the rest of the year. If you're growing bulbs that bloom for a short period and then die back, overplant them with an attractive ground cover such as snow-in-summer (*Cerastium tomentosum*).

Plan for a progression of interest throughout the year. In other words, don't orchestrate a spring or summer show and forget about fall and winter. A deciduous tree with a graceful branch structure looks lovely even after its leaves have fallen.

Affordable Luxuries

One advantage of working with a small space is that you may be able to splurge on some elements. What might be too costly on a grander scale may be within your budget for a small garden.

■ *Large specimens.* Give your garden a striking accent instantly by planting large specimens of slow-growing trees and shrubs—as large as you can afford. If planted from the commonly sold 1- or 5-gallon containers or, in the case of some trees, as bare-root whips, these plants might take years to reach specimen size.

This investment makes sense only for slow growers you want to feature prominently. Start other plants from small containers or (for annuals and some perennials) from seed; most plants actually become established more quickly if planted small.

■ *More plants.* If you want a ground cover—especially a slow-growing one—to fill in faster, purchase more plants and place them a little closer together. Be wary of doing this with other plants, however, or you may end up with an unappealing tangle.

■ *Improved soil.* If your native soil presents a pH or nutrient problem or is difficult to work (see page 88), consider bringing in new soil rather than struggling needlessly. If you have shallow clay soil and want to grow plants that need a deep, well-drained

Fine Points

Quality structural details are more affordable on the scale of a small garden. Bent willow chair, left, is a garden focal point in itself (Design: Robert Duranleau). At center, open-structured gate lets you see arriving guests (Design: G. Grismore, Inc.). Curve of brick wall, right, gracefully echoes slope above (Design: Woodward Dike).

growing medium, the solution may be a raised bed filled with an improved soil mix.

■ *Top-quality materials.* Paving and construction materials have greater impact in a small space than in a larger one—so the better the materials, the better looking the garden. You may find that top-quality material is affordable for a restricted space.

■ *Structural details.* When space is limited, you may be able to spend more on details that can turn fences, lattice screens, and other structures into design features. For example, frame a trellis with molding, or alternate board widths in a fence.

Putting Your Design on Paper

Sketch your trial design on an overlay sheet of tracing tissue placed over your site plan (see page 13). You can try out a number of ideas on tissue overlays, throwing away initial plans and starting over again without ruining the original site plan.

Start with bubble diagrams—rough circles or ovals showing space relationships. With your garden style or theme firmly in mind, draw "bubbles" to indicate the seating area, pathways, planting beds, and other garden elements. As you organize the space, pay particular attention to balance and scale (see pages 12–15). Think about how the elements will be viewed from the house and from different spots within the garden. Remember that your goal is to create the floor, walls, and ceiling that will transform your space into a satisfying outdoor room.

Once everything is more or less in place, you can fine-tune the plan, drawing in the actual elements to scale. Indicate seating areas, pathways, and any structures first, then concentrate on plants. You don't have to be specific right away: you can simply use descriptions such as "ground cover" (shade in the relevant areas), "flowering vine," "small deciduous tree," "perennial bed," and so on.

Next, decide on actual plants, taking into account the factors discussed on pages 27–28 and 78. Draw a circle to represent the width of each shrub and each tree canopy. Garden guides usually express the spread of plants as a range of numbers. Use the lower figure; the higher number often applies to the width attained only after many years.

You will be able to plant under most trees within a certain distance of the trunk. Planting is imprudent, however, if trees tend to grow surface roots or produce substances toxic to other plants; check a reputable garden book or consult local nursery personnel for advice on this score.

Your finished design is your working plan—your guide to installing the garden. Make one or two copies (large-size plans can be duplicated at many art supply stores); that way, you'll be able to take the plan out into the garden and refer to it as you work.

Four Views of One Garden

For any small garden site, there are likely to be a number of successful treatments possible. To illustrate that point, we gave a sketch of a nondescript backyard to four landscape architects, each from a different locale, and asked each of them to come up with a garden design.

We described the property owners as professionals in their early forties with two teenage children and no pets. The owners, we said, do not wish to make structural changes to the house but want a relaxing, beautiful retreat with plants that are in keeping with the local climate and water resources.

The yard is flat and empty, and there are some neighboring features that need screening: a second-story deck next door on one side, a shed abutting a back corner, a swing set and tetherball pole visible beyond an unattractive back wall. Wood side fences are in poor condition.

☐ *Waterwise in Southern California*

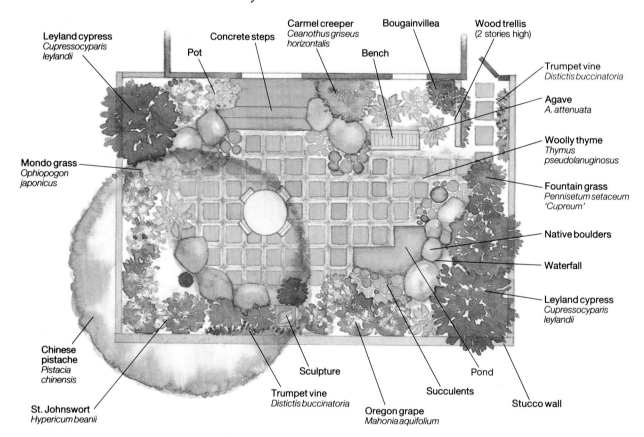

Leyland cypress
Cupressocyparis leylandii

Pot

Concrete steps

Carmel creeper
Ceanothus griseus horizontalis

Bench

Bougainvillea

Wood trellis
(2 stories high)

Trumpet vine
Distictis buccinatoria

Agave
A. attenuata

Woolly thyme
Thymus pseudolanuginosus

Fountain grass
Pennisetum setaceum 'Cupreum'

Native boulders

Waterfall

Leyland cypress
Cupressocyparis leylandii

Mondo grass
Ophiopogon japonicus

Chinese pistache
Pistacia chinensis

St. Johnswort
Hypericum beanii

Sculpture

Trumpet vine
Distictis buccinatoria

Oregon grape
Mahonia aquifolium

Succulents

Pond

Stucco wall

Local structural materials and plantings that need little water distinguish this Southern California garden plan. Space is "expanded" by visual height changes—a step-down patio (18 inches below floor level), a two-story wooden trellis on the east side, boulders bordering planting beds to hold the patio excavation in place. Plants soften boundaries and screen out unwanted views.

Details help make the most of the space. Woolly thyme is planted between the cut stone patio pavers, blood-red trumpet vine climbs the walls, and bougainvillea cloaks the trellis. Garden focal points are provided by a sculpture on the rear wall and by a waterfall pool.

Local materials include the flagstone paving and the native boulders; a stucco wall replacing the old fence is also in keeping with local style. The garden now has a single outside entry, defined and screened by the trellis. Design: EPT Landscape Architecture, Pasadena, California.

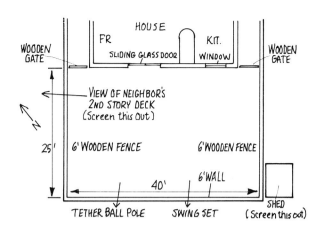

Starting Point

Here's the sketch of the lot that was given to the four landscape architects. From inside the house, you can enter the garden from the family room or view it from the kitchen.

☐ *New England Latticework*

An airy trellis-topped lattice corridor encloses the patio of this New England garden. Closely-spaced archway cutouts open inward onto the patio; a built-in wooden bench runs the length of the lattice on the southwest side. Vines adorn the overhead trellis, and a cutout accommodates a sour gum tree. On the southeast side, you pass under an archway to step down to the in-ground planting area; circular "windows" in the outer lattice panels here frame large hanging pots.

Dark brick header courses in the light brick patio surface echo the lines of the trellis enclosure. An unpaved section along the house is planted with flowering shrubs, daylilies, and periwinkle ground cover over crocus and tulip bulbs. Pots on the patio hold more plants.

A stepping-stone path wanders from the patio to a stone pool with bubbler, alongside a kitchen herb garden, and out the side entrance. Periwinkle carpets the ground, accented by bulbs in spring. Rhododendrons, a vernal witch hazel, and a kousa dogwood hide the next-door shed. Design: Carol R. Johnson & Associates, Inc., Cambridge, Massachusetts.

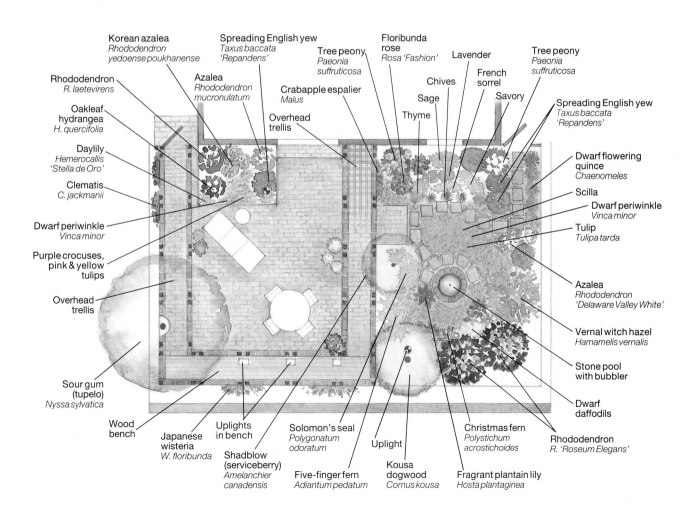

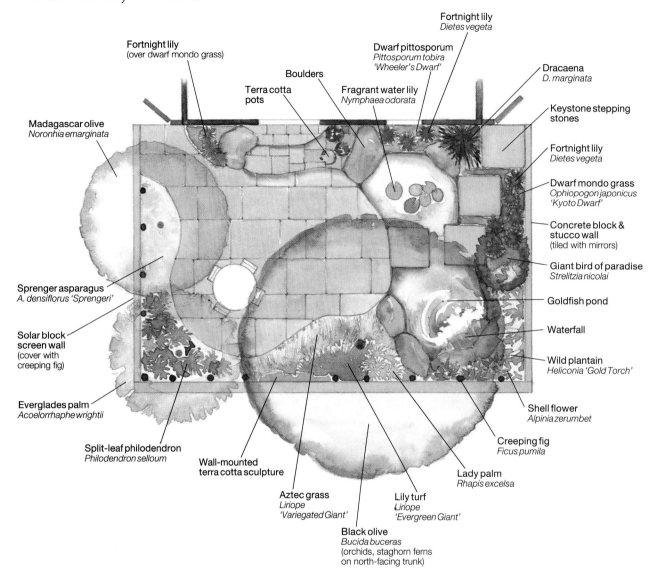

Fortnight lily
Dietes vegeta

Fortnight lily
(over dwarf mondo grass)

Dwarf pittosporum
Pittosporum tobira
'Wheeler's Dwarf'

Boulders

Terra cotta
pots

Fragrant water lily
Nymphaea odorata

Dracaena
D. marginata

Keystone stepping
stones

Madagascar olive
Noronhia emarginata

Fortnight lily
Dietes vegeta

Dwarf mondo grass
Ophiopogon japonicus
'Kyoto Dwarf'

Concrete block &
stucco wall
(tiled with mirrors)

Giant bird of paradise
Strelitzia nicolai

Sprenger asparagus
A. densiflorus 'Sprengeri'

Goldfish pond

Solar block
screen wall
(cover with
creeping fig)

Waterfall

Wild plantain
Heliconia 'Gold Torch'

Everglades palm
Acoelorrhaphe wrightii

Shell flower
Alpinia zerumbet

Creeping fig
Ficus pumila

Split-leaf philodendron
Philodendron selloum

Wall-mounted
terra cotta sculpture

Lady palm
Rhapis excelsa

Aztec grass
Liriope
'Variegated Giant'

Lily turf
Liriope
'Evergreen Giant'

Black olive
Bucida buceras
(orchids, staghorn ferns
on north-facing trunk)

□ *Tropical-style Florida Garden*

In an area where most residents originally come from harsher climates in the North, the preference is for low-maintenance gardens with a soft, lush, tropical feeling, according to the designer of this Florida garden plan featuring a goldfish pond with burbling waterfall.

The garden is tropical, easy-care, and functional—a multipurpose deck of local concrete keystone lets homeowners take advantage of southwest Florida's year-round outdoor climate. Large trees provide shade and screen out unwanted views. The eastern concrete block and stucco wall (typical local construction) is

tiled with space-enhancing mirrors. The western wall is made of solar block, a thin concrete block with patterned openings to permit air circulation. This wall and the rear wall are covered with creeping fig vine, its dark green color receding into the background for an illusion of more space and serving as a foil for a wall sculpture and lighter plants in front.

Native cap rock boulders give the pond an indigenous feeling, and keystone stepping stones cross the water; a recirculating pump powers the waterfall. Design: A. Gail Boorman & Associates, Naples, Florida.

☐ *A Northwest Natural Retreat*

Lavish use of wood and rich textural interest characterize this Pacific Northwest garden. Approximately half the space is devoted to a cedar deck, the rest to in-ground plantings. Each half has as its main design motif a Japanese fan shape—one of them created by the deck's 2 by 4s set on edge in a curved pattern, the other a moss garden bordered by stepping stones set in river rock. The moss functions as lawn but needs no mowing.

Part of the wooden seating area at the edge of the deck also serves as steps down to the moss garden. Vine maples mask views off the property, and a wooden trellis provides more privacy. One section of

the trellis zigzags above three basalt towers (2, 4, and 6 feet tall), the lowest drilled for a bubbler to create a recirculating fountain.

Lots of white blossoms are used for a brightening effect in what is an often-gray climate—masses of white bulbs and white-blooming ground cover under trees, white crocuses naturalized in the moss garden. White and purple-flowering vines soften the rear wall. Pots on the deck are filled with colorful perennials, and herbs grow in pots on the deck and in a new pop-out kitchen window. Beneath the window is a new garden storage area. Design: Harvard & Associates, Seattle, Washington.

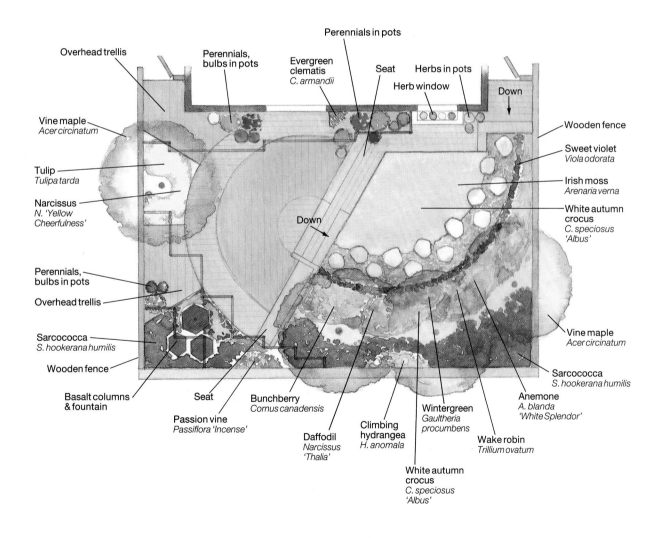

Perennials in pots

Overhead trellis

Perennials, bulbs in pots

Evergreen clematis
C. armandii

Seat

Herbs in pots

Herb window

Down

Vine maple
Acer circinatum

Tulip
Tulipa tarda

Narcissus
N. 'Yellow Cheerfulness'

Down

Wooden fence

Sweet violet
Viola odorata

Irish moss
Arenaria verna

White autumn crocus
C. speciosus 'Albus'

Perennials, bulbs in pots

Overhead trellis

Sarcococca
S. hookerana humilis

Wooden fence

Basalt columns & fountain

Seat

Passion vine
Passiflora 'Incense'

Bunchberry
Cornus canadensis

Daffodil
Narcissus 'Thalia'

Climbing hydrangea
H. anomala

White autumn crocus
C. speciosus 'Albus'

Wintergreen
Gaultheria procumbens

Wake robin
Trillium ovatum

Vine maple
Acer circinatum

Sarcococca
S. hookerana humilis

Anemone
A. blanda 'White Splendor'

Traditional Charm Updated

If you have only a small area for a garden and want a unified design that combines visual appeal with practical use, why not plant an herb garden? The idea harks back to the Middle Ages, yet herb gardens incorporate all the charm and practicality that today's small-space gardeners are looking for.

Whether planted in a clipped, stylized formal knot garden design or as an informal mixed border, herbs make a delightful central theme for a small garden. Many are fairly compact growers with subtle foliage colors, dainty flowers, and lively aromas that add understated charm to a restricted space. And because many herbs are useful as well as ornamental, you'll make the most of your site. You can look forward to snipping culinary herbs fresh to stir into the soup pot, or drying aromatic kinds to create your own bouquets, wreaths, and fragrant potpourris.

To get the most out of your herb garden, plan the layout carefully. Ask yourself some important basic questions. First, how much space do you have? Is there enough for a 12- by 12-foot knot garden, or just a tiny plot by the kitchen door? (As long as the area gets sufficient sun, almost any size will work.) Also consider how formal (or informal) you want your garden to be. Should it be a place to stroll and relax as well as a miniature working "farm"? Do you want to emphasize ornamental herbs, culinary herbs, or both kinds?

To help you sort out the options, the following discussion provides some basic information about herb garden designs, both traditional and updated, and planting choices.

Herb garden layouts. Your garden can be large or tiny, formal or informal—whatever fits the available space, suits your taste, and blends

well with the overall design and feeling of your home and landscape.

Formal herb gardens have their origins in the walled courtyards of the Middle Ages and Renaissance, where plants grew in orderly and geometrically shaped beds, usually bordered by low clipped hedges and separated by paths. One popular design, the knot garden, featured intricate, low plantings that interlaced to resemble a knotted rope. Benches often were pro-

Oval of dwarf gray sage encloses English and 'Hidcote' lavenders. Around the brick walk are golden sage, woolly thyme, more lavender, golden oregano, woolly lamb's ears, yarrow, and sage. Design: Gretchen Hall, Linda Bowers.

vided for sitting and taking in the garden's fragrance; a fountain, birdbath, or sundial sometimes provided a central accent.

A formal herb garden can be created in a surprisingly small space. There is no end to possible layouts featuring geometrically shaped beds, carefully laid-out paths, and plants closely trimmed to create a neat, orderly appearance. If such a garden will be the focus of your space, you could add benches around the perimeter and more plantings against any enclosing fences or walls.

In an area where two house walls or fences meet to form an "L," you might try a fan-shaped garden. Tuck in a small patio to provide a pleasant spot for relaxing and enjoying the view.

Any formal herb garden layout can be given a less rigid look by trimming the herbs in soft curves to retain their natural mounding shapes. The photo below left shows how a classic circular design can be modified and the plantings pruned for a "looser" look. Based on an old family stitchery sampler, this garden fits neatly into a 13- by 21-foot space.

When you design a formal or semiformal garden, be sure to include paths for access. Appropriate pathway materials include gravel, flagstone, and brick (the antique look of used brick is especially attractive).

If your space is very limited, or if you don't want the herb garden to be the *focus* of your landscape, you can plan pretty and productive herb "patches" on a miniature scale. For example, simply by adding a widened circular area at one point in a path, you can create a minigarden in the formal style. A sundial or small fountain surrounded by a ground cover herb might occupy the center; low-growing border herbs can form a ring around the area.

Three Formal Approaches

The classic herb garden includes symmetrical planting beds and paths bordered by clipped hedges, but even a formal garden can take countless shapes, as shown by this sampling of possible layouts.

Along a narrow side yard or other area, you can plant an herb border, perhaps mixed with bright annuals and perennials. A tiny brick-edged circular bed just a few feet across can be attractive and useful when planted closely with a variety of herbs. And containers of all sorts are perfect places to grow culinary herbs.

Choosing the plants. The grouping of plants known as herbs encompasses a wide variety of annuals, biennials, perennials, and a few shrubs that have at some time in history been valued as seasonings or medicines, or for fragrance. Your selection will be determined by the design you've chosen as well as how you want to use the plants.

Unless you're planting a very small area or a container strictly for culinary herbs, you'll probably want to choose herbs for both their ornamental and culinary properties. That means you'll need to consider growth habits, shape, foliage colors and texture, and flowers, as well as flavors and aromas. (On pages 27–28, you'll find a general discussion of plant form, texture, and color as related to garden design.)

For a formal or semiformal garden in which beds are defined by low hedges or borders, select herbs that lend themselves to clipping and have a dense, upright growth habit. Boxwood, though not an herb, is the traditional border plant for knot and formal herb gardens. Among herbs, possibilities for border plants include germander *(Teucrium chamaedrys);* English or true lavender *(Lavandula angustifolia);* dwarf lavender *(L. angustifolia* 'Hidcote' or *L. a.* 'Munstead');* rosemary *(Rosmarinus officinalis);* and santolina *(Santolina chamaecyparissus).* Of these, germander and santolina are the best choices for very closely clipped formal hedges. As a bonus, most of the choices listed have

delightful scents and charming flowers.

For a dainty low edging that's more informal, you might try culinary herbs such as parsley, chives, dwarf sage, winter savory, or even bright nasturtiums.

Planting beds—formal or informal—can be filled with just one or two types of herbs per bed, or with several kinds to emphasize differences in texture and form. In a mixed bed, taller herbs such as yarrow could grow at the back, with lower types like chives in the front. Herbs with foliage in varying shades and tones of gray and green offer pleasing contrasts and harmonies. The artemesias and santolinas have soft gray foliage; greens range from the silvery green of rue and some lavenders to the bright green of parsley. Such novelties as purple basil add striking accents. And, of course, the flowers of herbs such as chives, lavender, nasturtium, and yarrow add seasonal color.

For covering bare areas or underplanting individual larger plants,

several herbs make attractive and aromatic ground covers. These include chamomile *(Chamaemelum nobile);* jewel mint of Corsica *(Mentha requienii);* prostrate germander *(Teucrium chamaedrys);* dwarf rosemary, pruned low *(Rosmarinus officinalis* 'Prostratus');* creeping thyme *(Thymus praecox arcticus);* and sweet woodruff *(Galium odoratum).*

For general purposes, 12 classic herbs to plant for both cooking and ornamental use are basil, chives, dill, lovage, sweet marjoram, oregano, parsley, rosemary, sage, spearmint, French tarragon, and thyme. For fragrance and flowers, try adding borage, burnet, lavender, lemon verbena, nasturtium, and santolina to your herb garden.

Most herbs thrive in full sun and well-drained soil, with average garden care; some may be able to withstand prolonged periods without water. A few, such as chives, lovage, parsley, and nasturtium, will tolerate some shade; these need more frequent watering.

*Mossy boulders, a bamboo spout trickling water onto stone,
and a "stream" of river rock—a few carefully chosen details
within a framework of plants can establish a distinctive garden
style and suggest a much larger landscape.*

Making the Most of Your Space

A garden doesn't have to cover acres to bestow beauty and pleasure. It's just a matter of making the best use of the space you do have. By taking care in selecting each plant and deciding how to use every bit of available space, you can create a garden that satisfies your personal needs and taste—and captivates those privileged to view it.

In the preceding chapter, basic principles of good garden design were explained. In the following pages, you'll see how these space-enhancing techniques have been put to use to develop actual gardens. This photo gallery of garden ideas illustrates creative solutions for many typical small-garden challenges.

You'll see gardens that gracefully transform rugged hillsides, that billow over decks and bloom in window boxes, or that offer seclusion just a few yards from passersby. You'll see gardening space created on walls and overhead, in pots and boxes and raised beds. And you'll see the kind of details that turn a small space into a great garden.

Small Wonders

A beautiful garden is a natural wonder, no matter what its size or style. With thoughtful planning, it's possible to make a big impact even in a limited space—and the two side-by-side city gardens pictured at right and on the facing page show that dramatically different effects can be achieved in similar small plots.

Perennial Favorite

Perennial flowers in bright pastels turn a streetside yard into a miniature cottage garden. A few bricks suggest a path through the blossoms.

Ties that Bind

Railroad ties veer off from two-level deck, serving as a retaining wall on one side and raised bed edges on the other sides of the small lawn. For instant privacy, ready-made lattice panels were fit into frames on sills bolted to existing stucco-faced block wall.

Down the Garden Path

Instead of settling for a strip of lawn in this narrow, sloping city yard, the owner opted for a more fanciful treatment. Clipped boxwood hedges stairstep down to a precise diamond; containers sunk into the earth make for easy freshening of seasonal color.

Strips & Pockets

On many house lots, the entry garden is hardly bigger than a handkerchief. Narrow side yards may feature little more than garbage cans standing on a concrete path. Other often-overlooked strips or pockets of garden ground may border driveways or streetfronts. Landscaping small or odd-shaped spaces presents a challenge—but imaginative planting and attention to design details can transform these neglected areas into showcases.

Stepping Out in Style

Neat bricks, white latticework, and bright flowers on a window ledge and in a planting bed enhance this beautifully kept walkway. Plants enliven the view from inside, soften privacy wall. Design: Mark Scott.

Sidewalk Display

Colorful clumps of rose and yellow arctotis, cottage pinks (Dianthus), and blue lithodora greet passersby along the sidewalk and welcome visitors through the garden gate. For a rainbow-like effect, use at least three plants of each color.

Eastern Harmony

Oriental-influenced side garden harmonizes wood, brick, and stone with a rich tapestry of foliage and a dark carpet of ajuga. Walkway leads through gate to the small back garden shown on the front cover of this book. Design: Konrad Gauder, Landsculpture.

Small Jewel

Tiny garden fills a sunny corridor with colorful flowers and greenery. Yellow coreopsis and white Shasta daisies bloom at left; dense backdrop of vines sets off hollyhocks and hanging ivy geraniums at right. Design: Katzmaier Newell Kehr.

Up Against the Wall

Cedar lattice screen shows off pocket plantings alongside deck stairs. Behind the screen, stairwell serves as storage area. Design: Swanson's Nursery & Landscaping.

A Warm Welcome

Entry to a garden courtyard at front of house showcases exuberant color display.
Bougainvillea vines trained up both sides of lattice portico meet at peak of gable; a down
light mounted inside the pediment lights entry at night. Front door of house is beyond
courtyard and pool. Architects: Keisker and Wiggle.

Finding Space on a Hillside

If your home is on a hillside or slope, a retaining wall or walls will help you claim usable ground. Particularly when space is limited, such a wall can be the one way to create any level space at all for a garden.

A hill rising up right behind your house can be held back with a retaining wall, allowing you to convert otherwise useless land into a space that may be wide enough for a deck or patio. If your front yard is a rolling hillside, you might terrace it with a series of low walls, creating both a gracious entryway and a display area for plantings. In any garden, a low retaining wall topped with a wide cap doubles as seating—and if built from material that complements your overall landscape design, it will help unify the entire garden.

For a successful retaining wall, siting, design, and materials are all

Crevice plantings soften look of dry-laid stone wall; slight backward tilt and wall's weight give stability.

critical. Because the wall must withstand enormous pressure from the soil (wet or dry) behind it, the factors governing your choices can't be purely esthetic ones; the wall must fulfill basic engineering requirements. Simple retaining walls, less than 3 feet tall and on a gentle slope with stable soil, can be built by an experienced do-it-yourselfer. But if you're planning a higher wall or one that's on unstable ground or on a steep slope, you'll need to call in a professional—usually a licensed engineer. And for any retaining wall, consulting a landscape architect can save you time, money, and possible disappointment. Remember that most communities require a building permit for retaining walls; check with your local building department.

Site and drainage. As a general rule, locate your wall where it will disrupt the natural slope as little as possible. The safest approach of all is to avoid disturbing the slope, period: build the wall on solid ground near the foot of the slope and fill in behind it.

If you do build on the slope itself, the hill can be cut and filled, then held either with a series of low retaining walls forming terraces or with a single higher wall. In both cases, the wall itself must rest on cut or undisturbed ground, never on fill. Low walls are usually easier and less expensive to build than tall ones; and because they bear a lighter strain, engineering is less critical. Nonetheless, it's best to bring in professional help

for any wall—low or high—that requires extensive cutting and filling.

Providing drainage for both surface and subsurface water is essential. A shallow ditch or gutter behind the top of the wall collects surface water. To collect the subsurface water that dams up at the back of the wall, you'll usually need a gravel backfill; water can be drained from the gravel bed through weep holes in the wall, or directed around the edge of the wall via perforated drain pipes or tiles. Any hillside drainage system should funnel toward a storm sewer, ditch, or natural drainage.

Materials. Though you'll have to select a material compatible with the job's engineering requirements, you still have quite a range of choices.

Wood is one of the most versatile possibilities. Landscaping logs, railroad ties, and unsurfaced lumber lend rustic charm to the garden; finished lumber creates a smooth, trim look. Timbers can be set horizontally or vertically. Always choose a decay-resistant wood such as redwood, cedar, or cypress; or use pressure-treated lumber designed for direct contact with the earth. Wood does tend to limit the wall's size; the higher the wall, the more care you'll have to devote to structural integrity.

Stone is often used to give an old-fashioned look to a landscape. For low walls, you can lay uncut stone "dry" (without mortar or footings)—the stones' irregular shapes help lock them together. For higher walls, both cut and uncut stones require concrete footings and mortared joints for stability.

Broken concrete—pieces of former sidewalks or concrete slabs—can be treated like stone. The pieces look surprisingly natural when laid dry with rough sides out; higher walls will need mortar and a foundation.

Wooden retaining wall reorganized this slope into a flat, raised planting bed bordered by a gravel path. Hip-high wall brings blooms into easy reach for cutting. Gravel-filled steps, framed with 4 by 8s, lead to upper level. Design: John Herbst, Jr.

Brick walls enhance both formal and informal landscapes. Remember, though, that brick usually is sound only for walls up to 2 feet high, since each unit is small and the number of mortar joints is consequently large. Other masonry units, such as manufactured concrete and adobe blocks, are also suitable materials if reinforced with steel.

For a high wall where engineering is critical, *poured concrete* may be the only suitable material. The finished wall's surface need not be flat and uninspiring; lining the interior of the concrete forms with rough-sawn lumber, for example, will produce an attractive textured surface pattern on the finished wall.

Plantings. Once your wall is in place, you can greatly enhance its appearance with plantings. A stone or broken concrete dry wall looks almost like a natural part of the landscape when you work in planting soil and grow plants in the crevices between the stones, as shown in the photograph on the facing page. A planting bed behind a low wall can become a real focal point in the garden. And any wall, high or low, looks charming with plantings such as dwarf rosemary or English ivy spilling over its edge.

Unless you want to reserve the top for seating, you can also use your wall as a backdrop for container plants; arrange them against the wall in a row or group them in clusters of varying heights. A retaining wall also makes a fine backdrop for a long, narrow flower bed, whether it's a low raised bed or an in-ground planting. And even a massive wall can be softened visually when vines are trained along its surface to create a living tapestry.

A retaining wall can double as a raised bed for planting if it's designed with a recess at the top for soil or planter boxes.

Coping with Slopes

Gardens that slope downhill come with some special problems—soil erosion and difficult access, for example. But if your site is small, you can't afford to let hillside space go to waste because of such potential difficulties. One way to subdue sloping topography is to terrace it with retaining walls (see pages 44–45), producing flat areas for planting and outdoor living. Building a deck over the slope can be another approach to the problem. Simply adding a flight of steps can make descending ground accessible—and the steps themselves create still more space for gardening.

City Beauty

Terraced levels open up this steep back-yard. Steps provide access; containers and climbing plants increase the growing space and make the garden seem larger.

Upstairs, Downstairs

Retaining wall and wooden staircase create a rustic two-level garden in this steep city yard. Scrambling vines help tie the two levels together and continue the garden on up the topside wall.

Coastal Tilt

Wind-tolerant plants flourish on this exposed California coastal bluff—bronze New Zealand flax, blue fescue, English lavender, 'Modern Classic' bearded iris. Sandy soil was amended with nitrogen-fortified ground bark. Design: Sassafras Landscaping.

Big Box Garden

Hillside terraces for vegetables function as low retaining walls, an alternative to a bulkier and more abrupt single wall. These raised boxes are constructed of 4 by 6s, held by a vertical 4 by 4 every 6 feet, with a 2 by 6 cap. Soil in raised beds tends to warm faster in spring, getting vegetables off to a quick start. Design: John Herbst, Jr.

Step-by-step Gardening

Terracing with broad flagstone steps turns sloping land into usable garden space—just add potted plants and beds of colorful perennials. Ground cover spills down the stone treads to unify plantings and paving. Design: Katzmaier Newell Kehr.

Uphill Eden

Sometimes a hillside presents an opportunity, not just a problem. This winding flight of steps has become a thriving multilevel garden. Sea lavender and white snow-in-summer scramble between pavers; blood-red trumpet vine (Distictis) tumbles from trellis.

Succulent Color

Rosettes, clumps, and spiky swirls of succulents make for hillside drama, providing a long season of color from foliage and flowers without using a lot of water. Plants grow in raised beds which stairstep up the steep hill, constructed of railroad ties anchored with rebar spikes. Design: Dennis Shaw.

Window Box Gardening

Delightful viewed from both indoors and out, window boxes are the very essence of old-world charm. And if you live in an apartment, in an attached house in the city, or on a steep hillside, a window box may provide the *only* outdoor space available to you for gardening.

The classic window box is a long, narrow wooden container, but modern variations on the theme expand the definition considerably. Window boxes may be made of trim white fiberglass or gleaming copper. They may be custom-made for special circumstances, or built right into the design for a new or remodeled home. A window box may not even be a box at all, but just a wide ledge beneath a window where an everchanging array of potted plants can bloom.

Seen from outdoors, window boxes provide an accent that brings a house's whole façade to life. And don't overlook the value of using a window box to dress up a utility structure (such as a tool or potting shed) that can't be hidden from view on a small lot.

From an indoor perspective, window boxes bring color to eye level and help make the visual transition from indoors to out. Use them to underscore a beautiful view or soften a less than desirable one. To camouflage an unwanted view completely, position a lath screen or other panel a few feet from the window and perhaps add lighting from above, under the eave; the plants in the window box will become the focus of an entirely private "view" that shuts out the larger one beyond.

Expand the definition of a window box a little, and you can include other, similar containers that bring color into closer view. Wooden planter boxes or troughs along the edge of a deck or balcony both brighten the surroundings and provide a little privacy.

Dwarf French marigolds, nasturtiums, and lobelia brighten metal planter set into rail of deck wall—a window box without a window.

Ground rules. Proper installation, good drainage, and easy access for watering are the keys to a successful window box. Keep in mind that the box will be heavy when planted: water-soaked potting soil can weigh 80 to 90 pounds per cubic foot. For this reason, any wall-hung box must be attached with strong metal brackets. If you don't want to hang the box, you might opt for a larger, built-in planter or one that rests inside a built-in bay (see drawing on facing page).

Before constructing a substantial built-in box, consult an architect or engineer regarding local codes and zoning. Most building codes require that a window box on an outside house wall have at least a 2-inch-wide air space between the box and the wall. If the space is less than 6 inches, galvanized sheet-metal flashing may be required between the wall and box.

Boxes on decks can be set into specially built "wells" (see photo at left) or hung by metal brackets from a wide railing; many nurseries and garden centers offer boxes that can be suspended from deck or balcony rails.

If you use wood boxes, choose decay-resistant redwood, cedar, or cypress for longest wear; waterproof them on the inside. A simple homemade or purchased box may need only a plastic liner or an interior coat of asphalt emulsion. You can line larger built-in boxes with galvanized sheet metal; solder the inside corners, then coat the inside of the metal liner with asphalt emulsion to discourage rust. Make drainage holes in any type of liner in line with the holes in the box itself.

Water must drain away from house walls and foundations, so be sure drainage holes aren't too close to the back of the window box. For boxes set inside a bay (like that illustrated on the facing page), install a plastic or copper pipe to carry the water away. A piece of plastic mesh or a layer of gravel will keep soil from washing out drain holes.

Plant choices and care. A window box makes a good home for almost any plant of fairly modest size—annuals, perennials, bulbs, even some vining plants. Just make sure the plants you choose are suited to your climate, and that they'll receive the necessary light.

Like any container, a window box offers an appealing place to experiment with different plant types and combinations. A box filled to overflowing with one color or kind of plant, such as yellow-orange nasturtiums or tuberous begonias in a rainbow of hues, makes a dramatic focal point. Equally attractive is a cottage garden-style mixture of colors and shapes; for example, upright-growing pink geraniums might be bordered with blue lobelia trailing over the box sides. Foliage can provide color, too; silvery gray dusty miller or lush green English ivy contrasts beautifully with bright annual flowers. And kitchen gardeners will find a window box the ideal spot for a mixed "bed" of culinary herbs.

To keep window boxes looking good all year round, plan for seasonal color; follow summer-blooming impatiens with chrysanthemums in fall, then daffodils and violas in spring. In mild-winter climates, you can also combine summer annuals like marigolds with all-year foliage plants such as English ivy; after the flowers fade, the ivy will still look handsome all winter. For large built-in boxes, low-maintenance, drought-tolerant plants are especially good choices. Try dwarf lantana, dwarf oleanders, verbena, crown of thorns (*Euphorbia milii*), and coral aloe (*Aloe striata*).

Picture-pretty pots of orange and lavender violas sit atop window ledge (tiled for protection). Design: Kathy Yandell, Inner Gardens Colorscaping.

Cook's Garden

Planted with culinary herbs and geraniums, kitchen window boxes sit behind a false front sheathed in siding to match the house. Top trim is redwood. Plastic tubing at ends drains moisture from watering away from house wall. Design: Karl G. Smith, Margaret Simon.

Use good, loose, lightweight potting soil in window boxes; if you're replanting, work in enough fresh potting soil to make the mix loose and light. Keep the soil at least an inch below the box's top edge, and space plants closely. Keep trailing plants near the outside edge, upright ones at the back. If you apply slow-release fertilizer, you can greatly stretch the intervals between fertilizer applications.

An alternative to planting directly in the box is to fill it with coarse vermiculite, then sink containers (pots 6 inches or more in diameter, or gallon cans) into that. The vermiculite helps keep plants from drying out.

Frequent and thorough watering is essential for keeping window box plants alive and well. The job is easy if the box hangs directly below a sink-side window; if it's hard to reach or is in a very sunny southern exposure, consider installing a timer-operated drip irrigation system (see page 91). When you water by hand, use a slow-running hose or a watering can, and water thoroughly.

Vertical Gardening

Training plants up a wall or trellis adds space and drama to the small garden. Vertical plantings can bring abundant bloom or foliage to even a very restricted area—and training or mounting plants to grow upward has practical advantages, too. Vines camouflage or decorate walls that, if left bare, would detract from the garden. Espaliered plants (see pages 56–57) turn a plain fence into a work of art. And both fruit and flowers are easier to cut when at eye level.

Romance of the Rose

Carefully placed flower tower can accent a planting bed, create a garden focal point, and bring fragrance up close. For this rose support, ¾-inch reinforcing bars were welded to a 2-inch steel pipe bolted to a 2½-inch pipe sleeve set in concrete.

Floral Magic

Cloaked in vibrant red-flowered bougainvillea, this dressed-up wall blends harmoniously with the plantings below: roses, star jasmine, and rosemary trailing over a raised bed. Design: Katzmaier Newell Kehr.

Flower Power

Show-off begonias brighten garage wall with flamboyant color at one end of small garden. Begonias grow in wooden planter boxes secured to the wall.

Living Lattice

Rock cotoneaster crisscrosses fence, fastened loosely with twist ties to U-shaped staples nailed in place. Pruning after spring flowers and at summer's end maintains plant's shape.

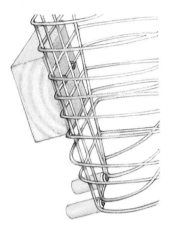

Wall Garden

Lobelia tumbles from moss-lined wire baskets on house wall, providing luxuriant bloom from late spring into fall. Containers are hung when lobelia is in full flower. A 2 by 4 block stapled to the back of each basket allows air circulation and prevents moisture from staining wall; dowels keep basket straight (see above right). Another option for wall-hung blossoms is to use clay pots secured with metal clips and expansion bolts (above left). Avoid walls exposed to drying winds, long periods of hot sun, or heavy shade. Water and fertilize diligently.

Blooming Trunk

Head-to-toe color from foliage and flowers greets visitors entering this cheerful front garden. Clay pots of impatiens are mounted to a tree trunk above a stand of agapanthus. Red-tinged Boston ivy climbs chimney.

Bold Climber

Triumphant trumpet vine (Distictis buccinatoria) climbs up house wall and balcony railing, lavishing its red bloom over a small brick entryway. Wires attached to eyescrews support the vine's upward spread.

Springtime Classic

Espaliered red-flowering quince is living work of art against burnished wood of house wall. Branches are tied loosely to small nails tapped into wall every 1 or 2 feet; branches that grow perpendicular to wall are pruned away. Choose flowering quince, not fruiting kind, for espalier.

Growing Geometry: Espalier

The intriguing form of an espalier lends beauty to a small garden all year. Even after the last fruit has been picked and the last leaf has fallen, the bare branches of espaliered deciduous plants create a bold, sculptural pattern against a garden wall or trellis.

Classic espalier was developed by 16th- and 17th-century European master gardeners, who succeeded in growing productive fruit trees in confined areas by training the branches into a flat framework. Today, the practice has expanded to include purely ornamental plants, trained both in traditional symmetrical arrangements and in irregular patterns determined by the plant's growth habit.

Espaliers are perfect for narrow planting spaces such as side yards, or for any wall or fence where you want a tracery of branches, foliage, or flowers. They can provide a strong garden focal point and serve as a freestanding fence. You can even train a container plant as an espalier by attaching a trellis to the pot.

Which plants are suitable? Dwarf fruit trees are the best-known choices for espalier, but other trees and shrubs also are effective; just be sure

the branches are flexible enough to train. The less vigorous the tree, the more easily it can be held to the rigid structure of formal espalier; vigorous types adapt best to a less structured design, such as an informal fan.

Espaliered fruit trees can provide an abundance of fruit in a small space, and they begin bearing at an early age. Semidwarf and dwarf apple and pear trees are the best candidates for precise geometric patterns, since they're easiest to train; both have pliant branches, and both develop long-lived fruiting spurs (short shoots that form flowers and bear fruit). Avoid tip-bearing apple varieties such as 'Granny Smith', 'Jonathan', and 'Rome Beauty' and apple trees on standard rootstocks. Trees on semidwarf rootstocks grow well on a large wall or fence; for smaller areas, dwarf rootstocks are best.

For an informal espalier, choose vigorous fruit trees or varieties that fruit on young wood, such as citrus, fig, persimmon, and pineapple guava. Citrus trees can also be trained into more formal designs, such as the horizontal cordon (see drawing below); for good fruit production, allow foliage to grow in thickly.

Apricots, cherries, and plums are more difficult to train: their growth habit is upright and their branches are less flexible. These adapt best to upright shapes such as the candelabra.

Choices for attractive espaliers aren't limited to fruit trees. Other possibilities include bottlebrush (*Callistemon*), bougainvillea, some camellias, some cotoneasters and podocarpus, pyracantha, sweet olive (*Osmanthus fragrans*), some viburnums, and vine maple (*Acer circinatum*).

Training an espalier. The basic idea is to direct branches along wires or a wide trellis according to particular two-dimensional patterns like those shown below. Branches that obscure the pattern are pruned away. Don't expect the full design to become clear immediately; it may take several years of diligent training. Fruit trees in par-

Popular Espalier Forms

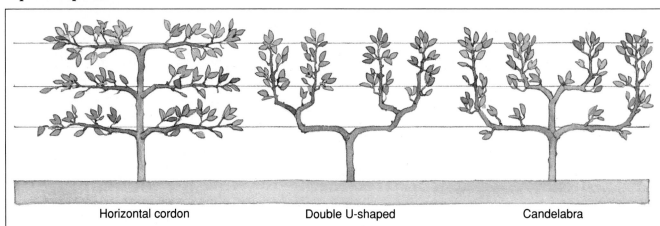

Horizontal cordon Double U-shaped Candelabra

ticular demand close, careful attention; when pruning, be sure not to snip off fruiting buds or spurs.

To support a freestanding espalier, use a wooden trellis or build a support of 12- to 14-gauge galvanized wire stretched between 4 by 4 posts. To train trees on a fence or wall, use eyescrews threaded with horizontal wires set about 18 inches apart.

Plant deciduous fruit trees during their winter dormancy; if possible, start with unbranched bare-root whips that have not been topped at the nursery. Plant citrus trees in early spring, after all danger of frost is past. In cool-summer climates, set plants in full sun. In hot-summer areas, avoid planting against light, south-facing walls. Position plants 6 to 8 inches from a wall or fence. Set them at least 6 feet apart for the horizontal cordon or candelabra design, 2 to 4 feet apart for Belgian fences or doublets.

For horizontal patterns, head back planted unbranched whips at or just above the first horizontal support wire, keeping two buds facing in opposite directions and one to grow vertically (if design calls for a central leader). If you buy a branched tree or shrub, select the two best branches be-

Trained in candelabra pattern, this European pear bears a frothy tracery of white flowers in spring.

low the first wire to form the first horizontal tier. Cut off all the other branches, and head back the main leader to a bud just above the two branches you've saved.

During successive seasons, you'll need to prune and train the tree or shrub according to your chosen design. For a horizontal cordon, for example, begin the first growing season by bending the branches you want to grow horizontally down at a 45° angle and securing them to the wire or trellis with plastic nursery ties; as the season progresses, gradually lower and tie branches, bringing them to a

horizontal position by the time the season ends. Train one branch vertically and remove all other shoots. During the dormant period, head back the vertical leader to just above the next wire; during the following growing season, select two new shoots to form the next horizontal tier as you did the first one.

Adjust branch angles (raise to increase vigor, lower to reduce it) so branches stay in balance. When lateral growth on branches reaches 12 to 14 inches, prune it back to three buds.

For diagonal patterns like the Belgian doublet, you don't head back whips at planting time. Buy whips with tops on, prune off any branches, and plant at 60° angles.

For an informal espalier, follow the natural shape of the plant, using your sense of artistry as a guide.

When plants reach the desired height, cut back the vertical or diagonal leaders to just above the top branch. Keep horizontal branches the right length by pruning back the ends to downward-facing side branches in late spring and summer. Keep top growth on older plants trimmed back to avoid shading lower branches.

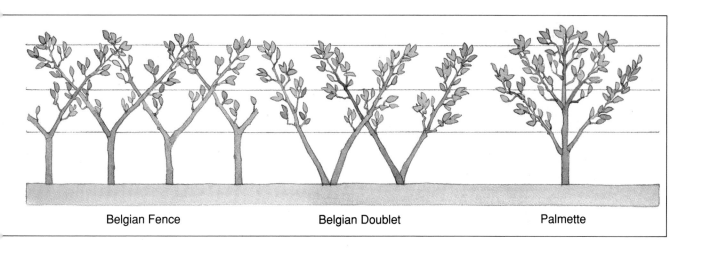

Belgian Fence   Belgian Doublet   Palmette

Growing Up & Over

In small gardens, every square foot counts—on the ground and higher up. Besides growing plants on posts, walls, or trellises, you can let some varieties twine overhead. Heavy, woody vines (such as wisteria) are favorites for overhead training. Such plants require a minimum of ground space; their leaves provide filtered shade in hot weather, and deciduous types let the sun through in winter.

Sheltering Arbor

Adorning a patio trellis, kiwi fruit takes no room away from the garden, adds a cool green ceiling and shade on hot days—and is easy to harvest.

Overhead Orchard

Fifteen buckets of apples are produced each year on this arbor, built for a narrow garden that lacks enough sunny space to grow the fruit otherwise. Supported by a 9-foot-high trellis, the branches of three trees soar above the shadows to flourish in sunlight. During summer, upright shoots are bent and tied; in winter, crowded branches are thinned.

Canopy of Bloom

Masses of white 'Madeleine Selzer' rose blossoms cascade over simple arbor, making a delightful garden entry with old-fashioned charm.

Storybook Entrance

You pass under a dense cloud of wisteria to enter this garden. Fanciful details—basketweave brick path, lattice-topped fence, and grillwork gate— accentuate the feeling of stepping into another world. Design: Bob Waterman.

Achieving Privacy

Small gardens often belong to neighborhoods where houses cluster closely, sometimes at the expense of privacy. But plantings, structures, and even the sound of water can help restore a sense of sanctuary from the world outside. And even when privacy isn't a practical problem, a garden bounded by a fence or a row of trees offers a comforting feeling of shelter.

Depending upon the circumstances, privacy can be created by open latticework, draping vines, masses of roses, or a high wall. When traffic sounds intrude into the garden, structural solutions are the most effective, but you can still soften the look of such a noise barrier with plantings.

Secret Garden

Streetside yard gained a private courtyard garden as well as studio space for the owners with the addition of a 20- by 20-foot wing adjoining the garage. New outer wall (below) is windowless to buffer traffic noise; wisteria and hardenbergia drape over a trellis to soften the effect. The 18- by 30-foot hidden courtyard (above) has a brick patio and a path of flagstones interplanted with woolly thyme. Garden design: Susan Sasaki.

Private Screening

Wisteria draped over trellis combines with ferns and other plantings to form lush foliage screen, softening look of privacy fence and providing textured backdrop for outdoor living. Sound of water further enhances feeling of privacy. Design: Swanson's Nursery & Landscaping.

Wall-to-wall Carpet

Adding a 2½-foot-tall stucco wall 2 feet behind existing retaining wall created privacy and a new raised bed for this corner lot with below-grade yard. Fragrant prostrate rosemary carpets the planting bed, brightened by daffodils in spring. Orchid rockrose (just visible above wall) screens the privacy wall on the street side.

Editing the View

A small residential lot is powerfully affected by whatever lies beyond its boundaries. If the scene over your back fence is a wild meadow or woodland, all to the good—but more typically, the view beyond the property line holds less appeal and may call for partial or complete concealment. Using plants and structures in a careful design, you can edit the view to hide negative features and frame positive ones.

Opening Up

A window in a wall can frame the best view on both sides and open up enclosed area, making garden seem bigger and more inviting. Lending a sense of discovery, this window links two patios. Design: Ric Wogisch.

Sheltered Spot

The earth around this Pacific Northwest patio was molded into a 2-foot-tall berm and covered with woodsy plantings, so now you look out at greenery instead of house entrance beyond. Fluffy spikes of sweet woodruff cover slope; azaleas add springtime color and fragrance. Design: Robert Chittock.

Looking Inward

With no views out from this property, the focus was turned inward. Tall pittosporum hedges frame the symmetrical garden, planned to be viewed from the main house level a floor above. Columns of nasturtiums rise from containers along the hedges, and a path of precast concrete squares leads to a garden-wide bench. Design: Chris Jacobson.

A Splash of Water

Water transforms a garden of any size, bringing enchanting sight and sound and perhaps even the refreshment of swims and soaks. Limited garden size doesn't rule out water in the landscape: you can still choose from features as elaborate as a swimming pool, as simple as a concave stone positioned so it will catch rainwater.

Potted Plant

One water lily in a pot of water can be a cool oasis in dry surroundings. Glazed ceramic pot was filled two-thirds with water, then potted pygmy tropical lily was placed on bottom; leaves and flowers rise on long stems. Half a dozen mosquito fish or minnows will control mosquitoes and algae.

Backyard Stream

Gurgling water and swimming goldfish bring delight in this narrow yard. Lush plantings surround cement streambed, pond, and recirculating waterfall (out of view to left). Design: Jolee Horne-Landscape Design, Grimes Natural Landscape.

Water Illusion

Interlocking plant and water boxes form a pleasing transition between deck and garden. Water appears to fall from top box, but actually it's recirculated from pond itself. Boxes are tongue-and-groove 2 by 6 decking faced with ¼-inch cedar, nailed together and bolted to deck. Pond has a 20-mil vinyl swimming pool liner on sand; black 6-mil polyethylene sheeting covers the blue liner. Plant boxes are lined with the black polyethylene over 10 inches of rocks and gravel. Water lilies and goldfish thrive in pond box; planters hold ageratum, impatiens, and lobelia.

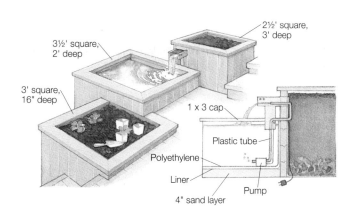

2½' square, 3' deep

3½' square, 2' deep

3' square, 16" deep

1 x 3 cap

Plastic tube

Polyethylene

Liner

Pump

4" sand layer

Gardens in Pots, Boxes & Barrels

Whether you set a single tub of rainbow-hued pansies alongside your front door or establish an entire patio garden of potted trees, shrubs, and flowers, container plants can bring life and color to any spot in your landscape. Even if your only outdoor space is a balcony or rooftop, artfully grouped pots and boxes can create the beautiful illusion of a complete garden.

Either by themselves or as a supplement to a regular in-ground garden, containers can provide instant color for special occasions. You can easily shift or replant them to suit the moment, or use them to fill in gaps in a border overnight.

Containers will also create privacy screens in spots where a hedge or tree won't fit. You might outfit a good-sized pot with a trellis to support a leafy vine, or plant a row of containers with tall bamboo to make a wall of foliage. Even hanging baskets can partially conceal a balcony or patio from view.

Display tips. For greatest impact, group containers together—the closely spaced blooms and foliage can actually hide the pots, giving your container garden the look of one large mass of flowers or greenery. To make the plantings look more like mounds than plateaus, vary the heights of the containers—arrange lower ones on the outside and taller ones in the middle, or raise some pots on pedestals (inverted pots or tree stumps, for example). Or use steps or a bench to create a tiered display. Including some tree-form plants in your collection also helps vary heights.

You can rotate seasonal potted flowers within a framework of container-grown foliage plants in various shades and textures, adding fresh nursery blooms or even a vase of cut flowers for special occasions. Container blooms can also be moved

around to supplement color in an in-ground garden; some gardeners sink pots right into the flower beds for instant garden refurbishing.

Choosing containers. There's almost no limit to the boxes, baskets, pots, and barrels available for planting. You'll find them made of unglazed clay (terra cotta), glazed clay (ceramic), wood, concrete, plastic, paper pulp, and wire mesh. (For longest wear, wooden containers should be decay-resistant redwood, cedar, or cypress.)

Deck stairs showcase 'Orange Ricard' geranium, marigolds, 'Amethyst' verbena, and annual chrysanthemum.

Consider porosity when you are choosing a container. Porous materials such as unglazed clay and unsealed wood help keep soil cool and aerated, but because they allow quick evaporation, they also make watering necessary more frequently. To limit moisture loss, you can line porous containers with plastic; be sure to punch holes in the liner to match the container's drainage holes.

Hanging containers may be made of wood, plastic, or clay. You can also line wire baskets with sphagnum moss and fill them with potting soil, then plant the baskets on all sides. If you do this, make sure to water often enough to keep the moss constantly moist.

Custom-designed containers can take almost any form that suits your garden, from pedestals holding a number of small pots to a bench with built-in containers at either end.

From a practical standpoint, any container you choose must provide good drainage. If it doesn't already have a drainage hole, drill one yourself or add a ½- to 2-inch layer of equal parts river or quarry sand and gardening or aquarium charcoal at the bottom of the container. Or double-pot—set a smaller container with a drainage hole inside the one without drainage.

To keep moisture from staining decks and patios—and to prevent the decay of wood surfaces—elevate containers to allow air to circulate underneath. Raise on bricks or wood blocks, nail cleats to the base, or set on wooden trivets.

What to plant. With careful maintenance, almost any plant can prosper in a container. For bright color, choose annuals and perennials; you can plant a single type or mix several in a vivid "bouquet." One easy and economical way to create such a container bouquet is to combine the seeds of compatible flowers such as bachelor's button, cosmos, and zinnia, then sow the mixture directly in pots. Thin seedlings as necessary.

When planting bulbs in containers, you can select an assortment with successive blooming periods for a flower show right through summer. Or create a striking seasonal effect: fill a single pot with yellow tulips, for example, setting the bulbs so close together that their sides almost touch.

Vines are another good choice for containers. Some offer attractive foliage (English ivy, for instance), while others, such as bougainvillea or wisteria, are appealing for their color and/or scent. Attach a trellis to the outside of the planter, or insert one inside before planting; or set the container at the base of a wall or post. Some vines will climb and cling on their own, but others must be tied to their supports.

When you're choosing container plants, don't overlook shrubs and trees. Their shapes and seasonal leaf colors, flowers, and berries bring year-round interest to the garden, and many look more dramatic set off in a container than they do planted in the ground. Container size, as well as vigilant pruning, will keep height and width in check.

For the vegetable gardener, containers provide a compact "field" for raising almost any crop—beans, carrots, cucumbers, lettuce, even squash, melons, and midget corn. For best results, select containers large enough to accommodate full-size plants, start with nursery transplants, and keep on top of watering and feeding during the growing season.

You can grow a hanging salad in a moss-lined, soil-filled wire basket (see page 75). Dwarf citrus and some berries can also produce well in large containers (try blueberries, raspberries, or strawberries). For more information on small-space food gardens, see pages 74–75.

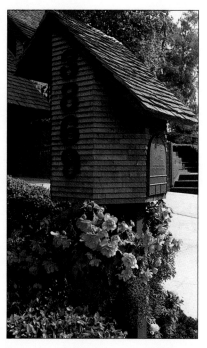

Begonia and lobelia blossoms overflow flat-backed redwood containers mounted to two sides of mailbox post.

Planting and care. Container plants need fast-draining soil that supplies ample nutrients. These requirements rule out most ordinary garden soil—it's usually too dense. For best results, use one of the excellent potting soils sold in nurseries and garden centers. If you're planting in hanging pots or setting containers in a spot where weight is a consideration, lighten the soil by blending 1 part vermiculite or perlite with 2 parts potting mix.

Start with a clean container; be sure to provide proper drainage (see "Choosing containers," opposite). Soak unglazed clay pots before planting so they won't draw moisture from the root ball. Cover drainage holes with fine wire mesh or pot shards; pour barely moist potting soil into the container.

Water plants well before removing them from their nursery pots to keep root balls intact. If, after taking a plant from its pot, you find that it's rootbound, score the roots lightly with a sharp knife and loosen them gently with your fingers.

Set the plant on the potting soil so that the top of the root ball is about an inch below the container's rim (to allow for watering). Fill in around the sides with more moist soil; press to plug any air holes. Gently water from the top, or set small pots in a shallow pan of water until the soil is moist. *For bare-root plants,* use the planting method shown in the drawing on page 91, positioning so the crown is level with the container rim.

The easiest way to decide if a container plant needs watering is to poke your finger into the top inch of soil; if it feels dry, it's time to water. In general, potted plants will need more frequent watering than those in the ground. To cut down on the time spent ministering to the water needs of your container garden, you might try adding water-holding polymers to the soil when you plant. Spreading a layer of stones, bark, rough compost, or gravel over the soil also helps retain moisture. If you have many containers, you may find it well worthwhile to install a drip irrigation system on an automatic timer (see page 91).

To keep plants healthy, apply a diluted liquid fertilizer every 2 weeks at watering time during the growing season (generally spring through summer); or add slow-release fertilizer granules or capsules to the soil. (If you start with a potting soil that contains nutrients, you needn't begin fertilizing until 4 to 6 weeks after planting.)

Note: Containers filled with an assortment of plants (rather than just one type) need extra fertilizer and more frequent watering to ensure good performance.

Repot plants when their roots look matted or poke through the drainage hole. You can repot in the same container, if you like—clean the pot, then use a sharp knife to shave ¼ to 1 inch off all sides of the root ball and score any tangled roots.

Decks, Balconies & Patios

If you live in a condominium, city apartment, or town house, your deck, balcony, or patio may represent all the "garden" you have. Fortunately, you can still produce a splendid miniature landscape by using containers and planters. If your patio or deck takes up only a portion of a bigger garden, it can become an intimate getaway in its own right when you add a display of plants and a place to sit and enjoy them.

Aerial Show

Containers of English primroses and fern asparagus hang above a Spanish-style balcony where breezes can gently turn them. Fairy primroses line up below. Design: Sandra Jones.

Balcony in Bloom

Just big enough to turn around in, this second-story balcony garden includes a ring of container-grown bulbs and perennials around a sunken patio with built-in bench. Plants are steadily rotated for fresh color. Design: Richard Haag.

All Decked Out

Adrift in bloom over a steep hillside, this deck provides the only available space for a flower garden. To make the most of a limited situation, the owners attached long planter boxes outside the rail. These are filled with a lightweight soil mix (changed every 2 years) and planted with annuals—easily tended through the deck railing. To add to the abundance of bloom, more container plants are set on platforms built into angles formed by the deck's zigzag design (see drawing at left).

Aboveboard Bloom

Wooden planter box overflowing with nemesia, ranunculus, and schizanthus forms deck "wall." Stout supports raise box 3 inches for air circulation, protecting surface of deck and bottom of planter.

Simple Solution

Deck plantings don't have to be elaborate to be effective, as evidenced by the simple lineup of red bedding begonias and yellow dwarf marigolds that enlivens this tree-high retreat.

Shaded Oasis

Graceful foliage of palms, ferns, clivia, and ficus tree softens and shades this tiled terrace retreat, creating a cool oasis around a central spa. Design: Mark Scott.

Floral Fiesta

Fearless use of color gives this all-container garden the zest of a Mexican fiesta. Massed impatiens combine with hosta and tree-form fuchsias; pots of small-leafed ivies hide bare earth under fuchsias. Plastic pots inside terra cotta pots allow instant switching of color as needed. Plants are started out of sight, then worked into the garden as they reach peak bloom. Design: Wanda Morken.

Planters, Pots & Beds

Many small gardens are restricted not only in space, but also in the quality or availability of native soil. For such gardens, pots, planters, and raised beds often offer the best (or even the only) solution to the problem.

Splashing seasonal flower color, serving up salad greens, or showing off a small tree, a planter or raised bed makes an exciting impact without taking up much space. And container-grown plants can also be clustered, suspended, or attached to walls above ground level to free up still more room. Turn to pages 66–67 for details on container gardening, to pages 18–19 for information about raised beds.

Prime Time
Concentration of plants at peak bloom time makes for a stunning display in this bursting-at-the-seams raised bed garden. Packed with cutting flowers and vegetables, foot-high beds enable gardener to sit while working.

Boxed Herbs

Wooden planter box built into corner of deck makes space for cheery display of flowers and kitchen herbs. Design: Swanson's Nursery & Landscaping.

Cool Hues

Blue hydrangeas, ageratum, and streptocarpus combine with ferns and Persian violet to create soothing color harmony in this small container garden at the edge of a partly shaded patio. Plants are raised to different heights for a full-mounded effect.

The Edible Small-space Garden

Think of a vegetable plot, and you probably picture sprawling hills of squash or long rows of bushy tomatoes and tall corn—real space hogs. But a vegetable garden needn't be large or spread out. By combining high-yield planting methods with space-saving techniques, you can pack a big harvest of vegetables (or even fruit) into a surprisingly small patch of ground.

Start by taking a fresh look at your yard. Is there a strip of ground

Garden space does double duty as luffa vines on A-frame trellis shade lettuce crop below. Trellis frames of 2 by 2s are hinged on top. Mesh concrete reinforcing wire is stapled to frame.

between house and driveway that's sunny but skinny? Using a trellis might allow you to tuck tomatoes or even melons into such a narrow space; or you could grow a handsome espaliered fruit tree there. How about a parking strip garden? In fact, why not think about your front yard as a spot for an edible garden? When the pole beans, lettuce, and tomatoes are combined with bright flowers and a few well-placed trees and shrubs, a carefully tended vegetable garden can look delightful.

If your property is on a hill, you can make planting beds for vegetables or dwarf fruit trees by terracing the slope with a series of low retaining walls (see pages 44–45). Remember, though, that you don't need a well-defined plot of land to grow edibles—you can tuck in a very small planting just about anywhere. You can grow a pretty and productive salad garden in a simple circle carved out of a lawn. Crops can also be slipped into a general landscape plan along with flowering plants and shrubs; some, such as lettuce and greens, can be planted in clumps among annuals and perennials rather than in traditional rows. Leaf lettuce, green onions, parsley, and many other herbs make a nice edging for a pathway or a bed of ornamentals. And vining vegetables and berries can be used as screens or backdrops when trained on trellises.

Even if your only outdoor space is a deck, balcony, or paved patio, you

don't have to forego homegrown produce—just grow it in containers.

Planting for maximum yield. One way to make the most of a limited space is to employ the high-yield French intensive method, a technique that encourages fast, steady growth and produces tender, full-flavored vegetables. The method has three basic principles:

■ Very thorough soil preparation, with all nutrients incorporated before planting.

■ Use of beds rather than rows, with each bed mounded above normal grade to form a fast-draining, well-aerated body of soil that warms quickly.

■ Close planting, so that leaves completely shade the soil at almost all stages of growth, reducing moisture loss and preventing extreme fluctuations in soil temperature.

A modified method, in which vegetables are closely planted in blocks rather than in traditional rows, can also produce a high yield. Both methods do require extra attention to soil preparation, but this isn't a formidable task when you're dealing with a limited area. You can liberally amend the soil with organic materials such as peat moss, compost, manure, or nitrogen-fortified wood by-products; you can also double-dig the soil to make it very loose and fine textured. Where the native soil is poor, planting in a raised bed (see pages 18–19) is often the best tactic—you'll start with good imported soil that's clean, fertile, and easy to dig. In fact, a raised bed makes an excellent growing area for edibles in almost any small garden; it's compact, it's convenient to reach into and tend, and it can be densely planted.

Besides close planting in well-prepared soil, two other methods can

maximize a small plot's production: double cropping and interplanting. *Double cropping* works for carrots, bush beans, and other vegetables that grow so quickly you can raise a second crop in the same spot as soon as the first batch has been harvested. *Interplanting* involves growing two kinds of vegetables in the same space at the same time; one grows faster than the other, maturing before the slower grower can crowd it out. Spinach, green onions, lettuce, and radishes are good fast-growing choices of crops for interplanting among slower maturing plants.

Space-saving techniques. When you don't have space to expand outward, the logical alternative is to go *up*. To grow sprawling, vining crops such as tomatoes, beans, peas, melons, cucumbers, and gourds, train them on trellises or contain them within wood or wire "cages".

Almost any trellis looks attractive once it's covered with lush greenery. Lightweight twiners like beans and peas can grow on a very simple frame—as simple as twine lengths strung in front of the porch or attached to the house gutters or eaves along the narrow area between house and driveway. Or you can build a wood frame of 2 by 2s, anchor it in concrete, and attach string, wire, or netting to support your choice of vining plants. An A-frame strung with concrete-reinforcing wire, for example, provides the strong support needed for heavy-fruited vines such as melons—and you can even use the space beneath to grow crops like lettuce that need shelter from too much sun.

Position your trellis with ends pointing north and south, so both sides will get sun. Dig a shallow trench (about 6 inches deep) along the base, then set in seeds or transplants;

Four raised beds and a strawberry ground cover replaced a lawn just off the kitchen to create this flourishing edible garden. Surrounded by gravel paths, beds are planted with lettuce, bush beans, carrots, beets, and green onions. Design: David Griffen.

keep the trench as a furrow for watering. As your vegetables grow, gently twist them around the wire or string, placing any wayward branches on the supports as necessary. Ripening melons and cucumbers may need support as they grow heavier; old nylon stockings make perfect slings.

To grow fruit in a small, narrow space, you can use the technique of espalier to train dwarf fruit trees on a flat framework (see pages 56–57).

Another excellent way to conserve space is to plant vegetables, berries, dwarf fruit trees, and herbs in containers. An all-container garden can include beans, beets, broccoli, carrots, cucumbers, lettuce, peppers, tomatoes, and even corn. Containers enable you to meet the soil needs of certain plants (such as blueberries, which require an acid mix) or to keep in check the growth of unruly plants (such as vining berries).

One novel approach is shown in the photograph at right; a wire hanging basket lined with sphagnum moss and filled with potting soil is planted with several varieties of leaf lettuce.

Leafy salad bar takes minimum space when it's grown in a hanging wire basket, like this mixture of leaf lettuces and red chard. Line basket tightly with moist moss and insert plants 5 to 6 inches apart. Fill with potting soil and plant more seedlings on top. Water and fertilize often.

*A small garden can feature a variety of plants and habitats.
Here, diverse annuals and perennials highlight both shaded and
sunny areas. White nicotiana, campanula, Japanese iris, and
petunias brighten shadowy spots. Design: Robert Chittock.*

Plant
Selection
& Care

*T*he time you spend planning your small-space garden culminates in what may be the most enjoyable part of the process: choosing the plants to fill out your design. The garden that has existed only in your mind's eye will finally become real.

On the next page, we present a basic guide to selecting plants for the small garden: what qualities to look for, what kinds of plants to avoid. This general discussion is followed by descriptions of specific trees, shrubs, vines, ground covers, and colorful perennials that embody the best small-garden traits. Of course, these listings provide only a sampling of good plants; for additional inspiration, visit nurseries, arboreta, and botanic gardens.

Because a thriving garden depends upon advance preparation and timely care, you'll need to know how to ready soil for planting, how to water plants efficiently, and how to determine your garden's maintenance requirements. Turn to pages 88–95 for the fundamentals of preparation and maintenance.

Selecting Your Plants

Selecting the right plants is one important step toward making your garden a success. To narrow the possibilities, consider which choices might fulfill your garden design. For example, if you want a modest-sized, roundheaded tree to screen your yard from a neighbor's windows, note the trees that satisfy these criteria of size and form. Once you have a group of generally satisfactory candidates, begin to make selections based on the plants' appearances and esthetic relationships within your garden. Think about form, texture, color, and year-round appeal (see pages 27–28).

Function and good looks do not, by themselves, assure success. The plants you choose must suit regional climatic conditions and water availability. Certain conditions in your garden will also affect your selections. For areas shaded by buildings, fences, or trees, be sure to use plants that prefer or at least tolerate shade. For a sun-drenched south or west exposure, choose sun lovers undaunted by both direct and reflected heat. Frequent winds will dictate the use of wind-tolerant plants, or windscreens or windbreak plantings.

Be sure to factor in the nature of your soil, too. If it's acid, you'll find it easier to select plants that prefer acidity than to amend the soil to accommodate a broader range of plants. If drainage is slow, avoid plants that demand fast or "perfect" drainage; these are better reserved for raised beds or containers, where soil quality can be easily controlled. For more information on soils, see pages 88–89.

After you've limited your choices based on function, appearance, and adaptability, you'll need to ask one more question: do your selections suit a small garden? Nursery personnel, garden books, and your own observations will all help you decide whether each plant meets the following criteria.

■ *Minimal litter.* Untidiness is more conspicuous in a small space than in a large garden, so avoid plants that produce impressive quantities of litter. Of course, the entirely litter-free plant does not exist, but you should look for those that offer little or no problem from falling spent blossoms or fruits, or at least take care to locate "messy" types where their debris won't litter or mar pavement or seating areas. Be particularly leery of trees that tend to shed leaves throughout the growing season.

■ *Well-behaved roots.* The best small-space plants have "good neighbor" root systems that won't compete aggressively with other plants for soil space, water, and nutrients.

■ *Appropriate growth.* Match a plant's expected mature size to the allotted garden space, making sure the plant won't be likely to outgrow its bounds and crowd its neighbors. With the exception of hedges, plants that need continual restrictive pruning have been set out in the wrong location. Also be sure you know how long it will take plants to produce the desired effects. To get slow growers up to size sooner, you might consider beginning with larger specimens (see "Affordable Luxuries," page 28).

Suggested Plants

In the following pages, you'll find brief descriptions of a few of the trees, shrubs, vines, perennials, and ground covers that are especially worthy candidates for small-space gardens. Most are easy to obtain in the regions where they thrive. Beyond good garden manners, the emphasis is on attractiveness—in flowers, fruits, foliage, and form.

You may want to set aside ground (or containers) for vegetables or colorful annual flowers. Aside from suitability to your region, there's little to limit your choice of these plants. In mild climates, you may be able to achieve a year-round rotation of cool- and warm-season types.

Many bulbs and bulblike plants enter dormancy a month or two after flowering; the foliage dies, then vanishes, leaving nothing but bare earth until new growth appears. Such bald spots are especially noticeable in a small space, but there's a way to enjoy your daffodils without having to endure a bare-earth landscape later: overplant the area with low-growing annuals or perennials that will provide color after the bulbs have faded.

Trees

Some trees are cherished for the shade they cast, while others are planted simply to provide a vertical garden accent. And one or more trees may be needed to screen a less-than-lovely view.

Whatever purpose a tree is meant to serve, it should not introduce problems that outweigh its benefits. Scale is critical: don't plant a tree with a 50-foot spread to shade a 25-foot-wide garden. Root systems should offer little or no competition to the other plants you'll be setting out in (necessarily) close proximity. Problems from pests, diseases, and litter should be minimal or nonexistent.

Finally, of course, the tree should look good all year long—even during any leafless period.

The following trees are just a few fine candidates for a small garden.

■ *Acer circinatum.* Vine maple. Deciduous. Hardy to −20°F/−29°C; needs some winter chill. This Pacific Northwest native is almost vinelike in the forest; in the garden, it's a multitrunked, slightly irregular tree to 35 feet. Broad, circular, shallowly lobed leaves are light green, turning tawny yellow to red in fall. Open structure casts light shade.

■ *Acer palmatum.* Japanese maple. Deciduous. Hardy to –20°F/–29°C; prefers some winter chill. Best under conditions that suit azaleas. Delicate-looking, graceful tree to 20 to 25 feet high and wide; round topped, with spreading horizontal tiers of branches. Deeply lobed leaves, 2 to 4 inches wide, may be yellow, orange, or red in fall. Surface roots outcompete delicate plants. (Illustration at right.)

■ *Amelanchier.* Shadblow, serviceberry. Deciduous. Hardy to –30°F/–34°C; needs cold winters. Slender trees to 25 to 30 feet, casting filtered shade through branches set with small, oval leaves. Good (but brief) spring show of white or pinkish flowers is followed by purplish new leaves, edible dark blue fruits, then glowing fall color.

■ *Cercidium.* Palo verde. Deciduous. Hardy to 10°F/–12°C. Desert gardens welcome the filtered shade cast by this tree's tiny leaflets, leaf stalks, and intricately interlaced branches. Extremely drought tolerant, but grows faster (to about 30 feet high and wide) and more densely with moderate watering. Abundant bright yellow spring flowers.

■ *Cercis canadensis.* Eastern redbud. Deciduous. Hardy to –20°F/–29°C; needs some winter chill. Rounded, with horizontally tiered branches; grows fairly rapidly to 25 to 35 feet and almost as wide. Clusters of small, sweet pea–shaped flowers in rose, white, or wine adorn bare branches in spring. Broadly heart-shaped leaves turn tawny yellow in fall.

■ *Citrus.* Evergreen. Included are the familiar orange, lemon, grapefruit, mandarin orange (tangerine), lime, and other hybrids; many are available grafted onto dwarf rootstocks. Hardiness varies, from about 28° to 20°F/–2° to –7°C; all need well-drained but moist soil. Usefulness limited to Pacific Coast, Southwest deserts to Texas, and Gulf Coast to Florida. Glossy leaves, highly fragrant flowers, colorful (and edible) fruits are year-round attractive assets. (Illustration at right.)

■ *Cornus florida.* Flowering dogwood. Deciduous. Hardy to –20°F/–29°C; needs some winter chill. Acid soil, regular water, light or high afternoon shade where summers are hot. Graceful, often taller-than-broad trees grow slowly to about 30 feet, cast open shade. Before spring leaf-out, 2- to 4-inch flower bracts in white (usually), pink, or rosy red cover the horizontally tiered branches. Small scarlet fruits follow, lasting after brilliant red fall foliage drops. (Illustration at right.)

■ *Halesia carolina.* Silver bell, snowdrop tree. Deciduous. Hardy to –20°F/–29°C; needs some winter chill. In good, deep soil with regular watering,

Acer palmatum

Magnolia soulangeana

Malus hybrid

Cornus florida

Citrus

makes a handsome specimen with arching branches; reaches 30 to 35 feet tall, a bit over half as wide. Pendant clusters of bell-shaped white ½-inch flowers in spring; yellow foliage in fall.

■ *Lagerstroemia indica.* Crape myrtle. Deciduous. Hardy to 0°F/–18°C; prefers some winter chill. Best where summers are warm to hot. Vase-shaped tree to 25 to 30 feet; summer flowers in foot-long clusters have crepe-papery texture, come in pink, red, magenta, purple, lavender, and white. In fall, the small, oval leaves turn tawny yellow to brilliant red or maroon. Smooth gray to light brown bark flakes off to reveal patches of pinkish inner bark.

■ *Magnolia soulangiana.* Saucer magnolia. Deciduous. Hardy to –20°F/–29°C. To enjoy this magnolia as a tree, you need patience—it will function for years as a large shrub, but eventually reaches 25 feet (or more) high and wide, usually with multiple trunks. Cup-shaped 6-inch blossoms (white, pink, or purple) decorate branches before spring leaf-out. Oval leaves turn brown in fall. Bare gray branches are attractive in winter. (Illustration on page 79.)

■ *Malus.* Crabapple. Deciduous. Hardiness varies; most to –20°F/–29°C, some lower. Among the many varieties are trees ranging from about 12 to 40 feet high, slender to wide-spreading, with showy flowers in white, pink, or red. Most bear decorative yellow, orange, red, or purplish fruits (edible in some varieties). (Illustration on page 79.)

■ *Melaleuca quinquenervia.* Cajeput tree. Evergreen. Hardy to 20°F/–7°C. Good at the coast or inland, with much or little water. May reach 40 feet; upright and open, with pendulous young branches bearing stiff, narrow light green leaves. Trunk has birchlike beauty: light brown to white bark peels off in sheets. Flowers (typically creamy white, but pink or purple in some trees) appear in summer and fall.

■ *Prunus.* Flowering cherry, flowering plum. Deciduous. Hardiness varies; most to –20°F/–29°C. The flowering cherries, usually modest in size (15 to 30 feet high), are noted for spring blossoms—white, pink, or nearly red. They need well-drained soil, some winter chill. Flowering plums typically grow 20 to 30 feet tall, bearing white or pink spring blossoms. Some have edible fruit; some feature bronze- to maroon-purple foliage in the growing season. Flowering plums tolerate clay soils better than flowering cherries do, and also like a bit of winter chill.

■ *Rhus lancea.* African sumac. Evergreen. Hardy to 20°F/–7°C. Established plants take little to regular watering. Narrow, willowlike leaves on somewhat pendulous branches give this open tree considerable grace. Slow growth to 25 feet, perhaps as wide; may have one or several trunks. Female trees bear small yellow or red fruits that can make a mess if they fall on paved surfaces.

■ *Ziziphus jujuba.* Chinese jujube. Deciduous. Hardy to –10°F/–23°C. Good in cool Pacific Northwest or scorching desert—tolerates drought and alkaline soil, though it prefers good soil and regular watering. Beautiful tree to 20 to 30 feet tall, with gnarled, somewhat pendulous, spiny branches; in warm-summer regions, bears edible, datelike brown fruit. Glossy, 2-inch oval leaves turn bright yellow in fall.

Shrubs

Shrubs serve as a permanent garden framework: they fill spaces, soften edges, and provide a backdrop for smaller plants. Those listed here are attractive all year, and all are of moderate size; they grow in orderly fashion and need no regular pruning if you allow for their mature sizes at planting time.

■ *Abelia grandiflora.* Glossy abelia. Evergreen. Hardy to 0°F/–18°C. Sun or partial shade. Small, oval leaves clothe arching stems on a rounded plant to 8 feet tall and wide. New growth is bronzy; cold weather also imparts bronze tints. Small, trumpet-shaped summer flowers in white or pale pink. Deep pink variety 'Edward Goucher' grows to just 5 feet.

■ *Berberis thunbergii.* Japanese barberry. Deciduous. Hardy to –20°F/–29°C. Colored foliage varieties need full sun for best color. Rounded plant 4 to 6 feet tall has arching, spiny branches covered with round, dark green leaves that turn yellow, orange, and red in fall and winter. Red berries in fall and winter. 'Atro-purpurea' (red-leaf Japanese barberry) has bronze-red to wine-red leaves; red-foliaged 'Crimson Pygmy' (hardy to –10°F/–23°C) grows to about 1½ feet high.

■ *Buxus.* Boxwood. Evergreen. Hardiness, growing requirements vary. The classic hedge plant has several species and numerous varieties, all with small, rounded, glossy leaves. Plants can take regular shearing but are dense and billowy if untrimmed. English boxwood (*B. sempervirens*), hardy to about –15°F/–26°C, reaches 15 to 20 feet (not good where summers are hot or soil is alkaline). Japanese boxwood (*B. microphylla japonica*) grows to 4 to 6 feet, is hardy to 0°F/–18°C, tolerates heat and alkaline soil.

■ *Camellia.* Evergreen. Hardiness varies; many to 0°F/–18°C. Partial shade to shade. Most feature glossy, oval leaves and showy flowers (autumn to early spring). Reticulata types and the most vigorous japonicas reach the size of small trees, while some sasanqua and hiemalis varieties are nearly vinelike. Reticulatas are rather gaunt, but all other types are fine foliage plants all year—for accent shrubs, hedges, espalier training.

■ *Escallonia.* Evergreen. Hardy to 10°F/–12°C. Partial shade where summers are hot. Small, glossy leaves densely cover solid, rounded plants; small, trumpet-shaped flowers in white, pink, or red cluster at branch tips in late spring, summer, fall. Height varies from 3 to about 15 feet, depending on variety.

■ *Euonymus.* Evergreen and deciduous. Hardiness varies. Two deciduous species (hardy to –40°F/ –40°C) feature rosy fall color plus showy reddish fruits. Winged euonymus *(E. alata)*, with oval, 1- to 3-inch leaves and a horizontal branching pattern, reaches 10 feet high, 10 to 15 feet across; variety *E. a.* 'Compacta', to 4 to 6 feet, makes a good unclipped hedge. European spindle tree, *E. europaea*, grows to 20 to 25 feet, can be trained as a small tree.

Among evergreens, *E. fortunei* (to –20°F/–29°C) includes shrubby and vining types, 4 to 6 feet tall. *E. japonica* (to 10°F/–12°C) grows upright to 8 to 10 feet.

■ *Fatsia japonica.* Japanese aralia. Evergreen. Hardy to 0°F/–18°C. Shade to partial shade, any but poorly drained soil. Dramatic, tropical-looking foliage makes this a garden focal point. Long-stalked leaves shaped like outstretched hands may reach 16 inches across. Stems rise from the ground in clumps, will branch if cut back. Small whitish flowers in fall, followed by small blackish fruits. (Illustration at right.)

■ *Hebe.* Evergreen. Hardy to 20°F/–7°C; best in cooler West Coast regions. Neat, rounded plants are densely clothed with glossy, narrowly elliptical leaves. Tiny white, lavender, crimson, or purple flowers appear in showy spikes at branch tips in spring, summer, or fall, depending on variety. Many species reach about 3 feet; several grow to 5 feet.

■ *Ilex.* Holly. Evergreen and deciduous. Hardiness varies. Sun for best berries, well-drained acid soil, regular water. The familiar "Christmas holly" types have spiny-edged leaves and red berries, but others have smooth-edged leaves and fruit in yellow, white, or black. Hollies vary in size from rounded shrublets under 2 feet high to bulky shrubs that will become trees. Most berry-producing female plants need a male pollinator nearby.

■ *Lavandula.* Lavender. Evergreen. Hardiness varies. Full sun, well-drained soil, little water. Lavenders furnish aromatic gray-green foliage and sweet-scented lilac to purple flowers in late spring or summer. English lavender *(L. angustifolia)*, growing 3 to 4 feet high, is the largest (hardy to –10°F/–23°C); dwarf varieties include 1½-foot 'Munstead' and foot-tall 'Hidcote'. (Illustration at right.)

■ *Mahonia aquifolium.* Oregon grape. Evergreen. Hardy to –20°F/–29°C. Grows well in sun where summers are mild; give partial shade in hot, dry regions. Glossy, hollylike foliage covers a dense, somewhat spreading shrub to 6 feet high. Conspicuous small yellow flowers in spring, blue-black berries later on. Bright copper new growth follows bloom; autumn leaves may take on purple or bronzy red tones. (Illustration at right.)

Picris japonica 'Variegata'

Lavandula angustifolia

Rhaphiolepis indica

Fatsia japonica

Mahonia aquifolium

■ *Nandina domestica.* Heavenly bamboo. Evergreen. Hardy to 10°F/–12°C. Sun or shade (at least partial shade in hot-summer regions). Upright, canelike stems and numerous narrow leaflets give bamboo-like appearance. Pink to light bronze new growth matures to medium green; cold weather brings red tints. White spring flowers may be followed by pea-size berries that turn brilliant red in fall. Some plants reach 8 feet high; smaller selections include 'Compacta', 'Umpqua Princess', and 'Harbour Dwarf'.

■ *Pieris.* Evergreen. Hardiness varies; some to –20°F/–29°C. Partial shade, acid soil, mild-summer climate. Elegant, refined shrubs have narrow, elliptical leaves—red or pink when new, maturing to dark green. Charming small white, pink, or red flowers in late winter or spring resemble lilies-of-the-valley. Various species grow 3 to 10 feet tall. *P. japonica* (lily-of-the-valley shrub) reaches 10 feet, with horizontally tiered branches and white blossoms in drooping clusters. (Illustration on page 81.)

■ *Pinus mugo mugo.* Mugho pine. Evergreen. Hardy to –40°F/–40°C. Sun or partial shade; well-drained soil. Growing slowly to 4 feet high, this is the one pine that will remain within the bounds of a small garden. Branches tend to spread, the tips upturned, producing a billowy plant.

■ *Pittosporum tobira.* Tobira. Evergreen. Hardy to 10°F/–12°C. Sun or partial shade. The basic species, a dense, rounded shrub with glossy dark green leaves, can become a small tree if not pruned. Cream-white spring flowers smell like orange blossoms; half-inch fruits split open in fall to reveal sticky seeds. Best for small gardens are 'Variegata' (to 6 feet high and wide), 'Turner's Variegated Dwarf' (shorter), and 'Wheeler's Dwarf' (to 2 feet).

■ *Rhaphiolepis indica.* India hawthorn. Evergreen. Hardy to 10°F/–12°C. Full sun or partial shade (denser growth, more flowers in sun). Dense, rounded, symmetrical shrubs boast good show of flowers from winter to late spring. Leaves are dark green ovals (usually glossy), usually tinted bronze or red when new. Loosely clustered flowers are white or pink; blue-black berries may follow. Tallest varieties grow to 6 feet. (Illustration on page 81.)

■ *Rhododendron.* Rhododendron and azalea. Evergreen and deciduous. Hardiness varies. Well-drained soil and regular watering for all, acid soil for rhododendrons and deciduous azaleas, acid or neutral soil for evergreen azaleas. Among the seemingly endless assortment are a host of fine plants for smaller gardens; visit local nurseries for recommendations. Rhododendrons range from almost treelike to nearly prostrate, with leaves from boxwood-fine to foot-long or larger and showy flowers in all colors but true blue. Azaleas are finer textured than most rhododendrons; blossom color encompasses white, pink, red, purple, yellow, and orange.

■ *Viburnum.* Evergreen and deciduous. Hardiness varies. Shade or partial shade in all but cool regions. Two evergreens (hardy to 5°F/–15°C) are particularly suited to the small garden; both produce showy metallic blue fruits. Slow-growing *V. davidii* may reach 3 feet high and 4 feet wide, with unusually handsome, deeply veined 6-inch leaves. Laurustinus (*V. tinus*) is an upright, dense plant to 12 feet high and 6 feet wide, with leathery 2- to 3-inch leaves and white flowers late fall to early spring. Shorter selections include *V. t.* 'Spring Bouquet' (to 6 feet) and *V. t.* 'Dwarf' (to 3 to 5 feet).

Vines

A vine can mask an unattractive fence or view, create a decorative filigree on a wall or trellis, make a leafy ceiling for an arbor, or—if trained upright on a post—serve as a simple accent. Most of the following vines provide colorful flowers in season, attractive foliage at other times. In particular, though, they offer easily trained growth that's unlikely to become a junglelike tangle, even if neglected.

■ *Actinidia kolomikta.* Deciduous. Hardy to –10°F/–23°C. Sun or partial shade. The foliage makes this rapid-growing twiner (to 15 to 20 feet) a sure conversation piece. Heart-shaped, 3- to 5-inch leaves may be green, green splashed with white, or green variegated with white and pink to red. Spring flowers are inconspicuous but fragrant. (Illustration on facing page.)

■ *Bougainvillea.* Evergreen. Hardy to 30°F/–1°C. Full sun. During the warm months, fast-growing, vigorous vines cover themselves with papery flower bracts in red, purple, pink, white, yellow, orange, or bronze. Some varieties are rampant to 30 feet, others fairly shrubby; all must be tied to supports. Heart-shaped leaves reach about 2½ inches long.

■ *Clematis.* Deciduous. Hardy to –20°F/–29°C. Roots in shade, tops in sun. Many large-flowered types are offered by specialty growers, some by local nurseries. Flowers (all with pointed petals) may be single or fully double, 4 to 10 inches across, in white, pink shades, crimson, wine, purple, lavender, or blue. Bloom time comes in spring or summer (or both), according to variety. Dark green, oval-pointed leaflets are set on twining leaf stalks; plants climb to about 10 to 15 feet. (Illustration on facing page.)

■ *Euonymus fortunei.* Winter creeper. Evergreen. Hardy to –20°F/–29°C. Sun or full shade. The various winter creepers are almost alone among vines in offering evergreen foliage in cold-winter regions. Rootlets attach firmly to wood, stone, or masonry, blanketing the surface in deep green, oval leaves to 2½ inches long. Mature plants bear decorative orange fruits. A number of varieties are sold; see page 81 for shrubby types. Common winter creeper, *E. f. radicans*, has inch-long leaves; 'Kewensis' and 'Gracilis' are smaller growers. (Illustration at right.)

■ *Gelsemium sempervirens.* Carolina jessamine. Evergreen. Hardy to 10°F/–12°C. Sun or light shade. Slender, twining stems reaching to about 20 feet bear a dense cover of glossy, oval yellow-green leaves to 4 inches long; a heavy crop of bright yellow, fragrant flowers comes in winter or early spring. Note: All parts of this plant are poisonous if ingested.

■ *Hardenbergia.* Evergreen. Hardiness varies. Full sun where summers are mild, partial shade in hotter regions. Twines at a moderate rate to about 10 feet; clustered sweet pea–type blossoms make a good show in late winter, early spring. *H. violacea* (hardy to 20°F/–7°C) has slender 2- to 4-inch leaves and lavender, violet, rose, or white blooms. The more delicate-textured *H. comptoniana* (hardy to about 25°F/–4°C) has blue-violet flowers.

■ *Hibbertia scandens.* Guinea gold vine. Evergreen. Hardy to 30°F/–1°C. Sun (but not reflected heat) or partial shade. Vigorous but not rampant, this graceful vine twines to about 10 feet. Handsome leaves are glossy, oval, dark green, to 3 inches long; yellow blossoms mid-spring to fall resemble single roses.

■ *Lonicera.* Honeysuckle. Semievergreen to deciduous. Hardiness varies. Sun to partial shade. Many honeysuckles are *too* vigorous, requiring frequent pruning. These four, however, are more restrained, reaching about 15 feet: *L. heckrottii* (gold flame honeysuckle), *L. henryi*, and *L. periclymenum* 'Serotina' (all hardy to –20°F/–29°C); and red-flowered *L.* 'Dropmore Scarlet' (to –40°F/–40°C). All have tubular blossoms from spring or summer into fall.

■ *Mandevilla laxa.* Chilean jasmine. Deciduous. Hardy to 10°F/–12°C. Full sun. Summer perfume of white, trumpet-shaped, clustered blooms evokes gardenias rather than jasmine. Twining vines to 15 feet have deep green, oval 6-inch leaves.

■ *Rosa.* Rose. Evergreen and deciduous. Hardiness varies. The so-called "climbing roses" are longtime favorite adornments for fences, arbors, and pergolas. Flower size, style, and color vary greatly. Most will survive winter unprotected (and with some foliage) down to about 10°F/–12°C; some can take yet lower temperatures. (Illustration at right.)

■ *Solanum jasminoides.* Potato vine. Evergreen to partially deciduous. Hardy to 15°F/–9°C. Sun to partial shade. The starlike white flowers resemble potato blossoms, hence the common name. Vines bloom throughout the year when weather is mild. Arrow-shaped leaves to 3 inches long are green or tinted with purple. This vine is capable of reaching 30 feet; needs periodic thinning, but worth the extra attention for its beauty and long bloom season.

Clematis hybrid

Actinidia kolomikta

Trachelospermum jasminoides

Rosa hybrid

Euonymus fortunei 'Gracilis'

Hemerocallis

Helleborus
orientalis

Aquilegia

Paeonia

Bergenia crassifolia

■ *Trachelospermum jasminoides.* Star jasmine, Confederate jasmine. Evergreen. Hardy to 20°F/–7°C. Sun where summers are mild, partial shade in hotter regions. Pinwheel-shaped, jasmine-scented white blossoms cover this handsome plant from late spring well into summer. Oval 3-inch leaves are glossy green, leathery. Given vertical support, stems will twine to 20 feet; without support, plant makes an excellent ground cover. (Illustration on page 83.)

Perennials

Perennial plants are garden mainstays for seasonal color that needn't be replaced each year. Though most need dividing and replanting after a period of years, some are as permanent as shrubs. The perennials profiled here are garden assets throughout several seasons, offering attractive foliage in addition to floral display.

■ *Achillea.* Yarrow. Evergreen. Hardy to –30°F/–34°C. Full sun. Yarrows include low, spreading plants and upright, clump-forming kinds to 5 feet. All have finely divided, almost fernlike leaves and flattened heads of tiny flowers in summer. Widely sold are varieties of *A. filipendulina* (fernleaf yarrow)—such as 'Gold Plate' (5 feet) and 'Coronation Gold' (3 feet)—and lemon yellow, 1½-foot *A.* 'Moonshine'.

■ *Agapanthus.* Lily-of-the-Nile. Evergreen. Hardy to 10°F/–12°C. Full sun or partial shade. Stems bearing large balls of tubular blue or white flowers rise above fountainlike clumps of strap-shaped green leaves. Tallest species is *A. orientalis*, with stems to 5 feet; shortest is 'Peter Pan', about 1½ feet tall.

■ *Aquilegia.* Columbine. Evergreen. Hardy to –20°F/–29°C. Sun to partial or light shade. Handsome gray-green foliage looks a bit like maidenhair fern: each leaf is divided into many rounded leaflets. Distinctively shaped flowers on stems 1½ to 3 feet tall (or taller) come in white, yellow, pink, red, purple, lavender, blue, and combinations. You'll need to replace plants in 3 or 4 years. (Illustration at left.)

■ *Artemisia.* Deciduous. Hardiness varies. Full sun, moderate watering. Usually grown for their foliage—typically gray or gray-green, but nearly white in two of the most useful: 3-foot-tall silver king artemisia (*A. ludoviciana albula*) and angel's hair (*A. schmidtiana*), to 2 feet (both hardy to –30°F/–34°C).

■ *Bergenia.* Evergreen. Most are hardy to –30°/–34°C. Shade or partial shade; sun where summers are cool. Flowers are a bonus; it's the foliage that counts here. Leathery, rounded, glossy green leaves may reach 8 inches across and 1 foot long, growing in clumps from slowly spreading, thick rootstocks. Most common is winter-blooming bergenia, *B. crassifolia*, carrying its pink to purplish flowers above 20-inch foliage. (Illustration at left.)

■ *Coreopsis.* Semievergreen and deciduous. Hardy to –30°F/–34°C. Full sun. Bountiful display of bright yellow daisy flowers all summer long. *C. auriculata* 'Nana' forms spreading clumps of slender leaves to 6 inches high; *C. grandiflora* reaches about 2 feet. *C. verticillata* grows about 3 feet tall; named selections include 'Moonbeam' (pale yellow) and 'Zagreb' (deep yellow), both reaching only 2 feet or less.

■ *Dietes.* Fortnight lily. Evergreen. Hardy to 15°F/–9°C. Sun or light shade. Both foliage and flowers bear witness to the close relationship to iris. Clumps of narrow, sword-shaped, 2- to 3-foot leaves send up slender, branching stems displaying six-petaled white or yellow flowers marked in other colors. Plants bloom for much of the year.

■ *Gaura lindheimeri.* Evergreen. Hardy to –10°F/–23°C. Full sun. Here is a long-blooming perennial (late spring into autumn) at home in hot-summer regions. Plants are shrubby, 2 to 3 feet high, composed of numerous wiry stems and narrow leaves, with wands of pink-budded, starry white blossoms rising above. Deep-rooted plants never need dividing, tolerate drought, thrive on just moderate watering.

■ *Geranium.* Cranesbill. Semievergreen and deciduous. Hardy to –30°F/–34°C. Best in full sun. The true geraniums (as opposed to *Pelargonium,* the common garden "geranium") are mounding to spreading plants with roundish, long-stalked leaves and clustered summer flowers of white, blue, lilac, or pink. These are excellent foreground and "filler" plants; larger ones make good specimens or drifts in mixed perennial plantings. Specialists offer many species and varieties; popular *G. endressii* 'Wargrave Pink' grows to 2 feet tall, 3 feet wide, with pink blooms.

■ *Helleborus.* Hellebore. Evergreen. Hardiness varies. Shade or partial shade. These elegant plants have bold, palmate leaves that look good all year. Clustered 2- to 2½-inch-wide, winter to spring flowers resemble single roses in white, greenish white, or purplish hues. Good choices include Christmas rose (*H. niger*) and Lenten rose (*H. orientalis),* both to 1½ feet tall and hardy to –30°F/–34°C, and Corsican hellebore (*H. lividus corsicus),* to 3 feet and hardy to 5°F/–15°C. (Illustration on facing page.)

■ *Hemerocallis.* Daylily. Evergreen, semievergreen, and deciduous. Hardy to –35°F/–37°C; deciduous kinds are better adapted to coldest regions. Best flowering in full sun. In late spring, branched stalks rise above fountainlike clumps of bright green leaves to bear lilylike flowers in a wide color range. Each flower lasts just one day, and all blooms will face the sun if sunlight strikes the plant from just one direction. Height varies by variety, from about 1 to 4 feet. (Illustration on facing page.)

■ *Heuchera.* Coral bells. Evergreen. Hardy to –30°F/–34°C. Full sun where summers are mild, partial shade in hot-summer regions. Good-looking foliage

and long spring-through-summer flowering season make this a favorite border and edging perennial. Above low, rounded, slowly spreading clumps of scallop-edged round leaves rise clouds of bell-shaped blossoms in pink, red, white, or chartreuse.

■ *Hosta.* Plantain lily, funkia. Deciduous. Hardy to –35°F/–37°C. Shade or partial shade. Virtually un-equalled for foliage beauty; the white or lavender flowers are secondary. Growth habit is always the same—clumps of overlapping smooth-edged leaves—but leaf shape varies from lance-shaped to round, plant height from 6 inches to 3 feet. Foliage colors include silver-gray, blue-green, chartreuse, and combinations. Watch out for slugs and snails.

■ *Iris.* Evergreen and deciduous. Hardiness varies. Besides the familiar tall bearded sorts in an array of colors, two other types are standouts for semiperma-nent plantings that look good throughout the growing season. Siberian irises (hardy to –30°F/–34°C), best in sun or light shade, form tall, grasslike clumps that last through summer; graceful flowers may be white, cream, pink, lilac, blue, purple, or wine-red. For full or partial shade, try the gladwin iris, *I. foetidissima* (hardy to 0°F/–18°C), featuring broader, glossy swordlike leaves and blooms of tan, blue-gray, or pale yellow followed by seed capsules that split in fall to reveal red-orange seeds.

■ *Nepeta faassenii.* Catmint. Semievergreen or deciduous. Hardy to –35°F/–37°C. This first-rate border "filler" is a densely branching, spreading plant 1 to 2 feet tall. Its oval, aromatic leaves are gray-green; small, lavender blue blossoms start in spring, continue through summer. Named selections include 'Six Hills Giant' (2 to 3 feet).

■ *Paeonia.* Peony. Deciduous. Hardy to –50°/–46°C; needs subfreezing winter temperatures. Full sun. The herbaceous peonies offer spectacular silk- or satin-textured flowers on handsome shrubby plants with large, segmented leaves. Each spring, numerous stems rise from perennial roots, developing into rounded clumps to 4 feet high. Blossoms up to 10 inches across come in white, pink, red, mahogany, cream, or light yellow. (Illustration on facing page.)

■ *Penstemon gloxinioides.* Border penstemon. Evergreen. Hardy to 15°F/–9°C. Full sun; partial shade in hot-summer regions. Upright, shrubby 2- to 4-foot plants have bright green, lance-shaped leaves and spikes of showy, thimble-shaped, 2-inch blossoms at stem tips in late spring or early summer. Colors include white, pink, red, violet, and lilac.

■ *Salvia.* Sage. Evergreen and deciduous. Hardy to –20°F/–29°C. Full sun. Vibrant blues are common to the perennial sages. These two furnish color over a long period: *S. azurea grandiflora* (upright to 5 feet, with spikes of brilliant blue flowers from midsummer into fall) and *S. superba* (compact 2-foot clumps with spikes of violet-blue blossoms all summer).

Arctostaphylos
uva-ursi

Lamium
maculatum
'Beacon Silver'

Pachysandra
terminalis
'Variegata'

Teucrium
chamaedrys

Osteospermum
fruticosum

Ajuga reptans

■ *Sedum.* Stonecrop. Deciduous. Hardy to −35°F/ −37°C. Full sun. Two similar species provide attractive, bushy foliage in spring and summer, flowers in fall. *S. spectabile,* to 1½ feet, has rounded, rubbery, gray-green leaves and tiny star-shaped pink flowers in broad, flat-topped clusters. *S. telephium* has narrower leaves, larger flower clusters; popular *S.* 'Autumn Joy' is sometimes sold as a named selection.

Ground Covers

Some of the garden's most useful though often unsung plants fall into the prosaic-sounding category of ground covers. All offer an alternative to bare earth (or lawn) without obstructing the view; all provide interest from foliage colors and patterns, and often from flowers as well. Besides good looks, the plants listed here offer good behavior: they're vigorous, but not likely to run rampant. For ground covers to use between pavers, see pages 24–25.

■ *Ajuga reptans.* Carpet bugle. Evergreen perennial. Hardy to −30°F/−34°C. Spreads by runners to form a carpet of dark green, somewhat quilted-looking foliage; rounded leaves may reach 2 inches across in sun, 4 inches across in shade. Conspicuous spring and early summer show of small, tubular blue flowers on 6- to 9-inch spikes. Many named varieties are sold; leaves may be bronze to purplish, variegated or extra-large. (Illustration at left.)

■ *Arctostaphylos uva-ursi.* Bearberry, kinnikinnick. Evergreen shrub. Hardy to −40°F/−40°C. Well-drained, acid to neutral soil. Full sun except where summers are hot. Spreading stems root where they touch soil, forming a dense, foot-high cover of glossy, inch-long, oval bright green leaves that turn red in winter. Year-round neat appearance is enhanced by white or pink blossoms in early spring, followed by bright red to pink fruits. (Illustration at left.)

■ *Armeria maritima.* Common thrift, sea pink. Evergreen perennial. Hardy to −35°F/−37°C. Individual plants form clumps of chivelike, 6-inch-tall leaves that make a grassy ground cover when set close together in a sunny location. Tight, rounded clusters of white to pink flowers rise above foliage; in mild-summer regions, plants may bloom all year.

■ *Campanula.* Bellflower. Evergreen perennial. Hardiness varies. Partial shade in all but mild-summer regions. Two ground-cover campanulas have a delicate appearance that masks their toughness. Dalmatian bellflower (*C. portenschlagiana,* often sold as *C. muralis*) forms a rounded mass to 7 inches high; blue-violet, bell-shaped flowers cover the rounded leaves from mid-spring through summer (hardy to −20°/ −29°C). Serbian bellflower (*C. poscharskyana*) has larger, heart-shaped leaves and star-shaped lavender-blue blooms on stems to 1 foot (hardy to −30°F/−34°C).

■ *Cerastium tomentosum.* Snow-in-summer. Evergreen perennial. Hardy to –40°F/–40°C. Full sun. Narrow leaves no more than an inch long are silvery gray, forming a dense foliage mat 6 to 8 inches high; in early summer, leaves are nearly obscured by masses of small snow white flowers. After bloom, shear off flower stems for neat appearance.

■ *Convallaria majalis.* Lily-of-the-valley. Deciduous perennial. Hardy to –40°F/–40°C; needs some winter chill. Light to deep shade. A favorite cut flower for generations, lily-of-the-valley blooms in early spring, its 6- to 8-inch stems bearing pendant white bells with a memorable fragrance. Massed together, the plants make a handsome ground cover with 8-inch, lance-shaped leaves. Plantings spread slowly from underground rootstocks, growing well even in competition with tree or shrub roots.

■ *Euonymus fortunei.* Winter creeper. Evergreen woody vine. Hardy to –20°F/–29°C. Sun or shade. Among the varieties of winter creeper (see also "Vines," page 82), two are restrained enough to serve as small-scale ground covers. Both have polished, oval leaves, trailing or creeping stems, general neat appearance. 'Gracilis' has inch-long variegated leaves; 'Kewensis' (sometimes sold as 'Minima') has solid green leaves only ¼ inch long. Both may take several years to form a solid cover.

■ *Gazania.* Evergreen perennial. Hardy to 20°F/–7°C. In a sunny spot, gazanias are virtually unexcelled for amount and variety of color. Daisy flowers, 3 to 4 inches across, come in yellow, orange, red, copper, pink, cream, and white. Leaves are typically long and narrow, green on top and gray beneath. In mild regions, plants will bloom off and on throughout the year; flowers usually open only on sunny days, close in evening. Some gazanias form compact clumps—good for massing in small areas—and others spread by trailing runners.

■ *Lamium maculatum.* Dead nettle. Evergreen to deciduous perennial. Hardy to –20°F/–29°C. Variegated forms are good for brightening up shaded areas. Sprawling stems root as they spread, bearing heart-shaped, furry-textured leaves to 2 inches long. 'Variegatum' features dark green leaves with a white central stripe; 'Beacon Silver' is almost solid silver-gray. In late spring or early summer, small, hooded flowers (usually pink) rise on short spikes. (Illustration on facing page.)

■ *Laurentia fluviatilis* (sometimes sold as *Isotoma fluviatilis*). Blue star creeper. Evergreen perennial. Hardy to 10°F/–12°C. Full sun in mild climates, light shade in hot-summer areas. For Western gardens, this ground-hugging plant provides a mosslike effect as it blankets the soil, flows around stones, or fills in between paving units. In late spring and summer, the tiny green leaves are all but covered with small, star-shaped light blue flowers.

■ *Liriope* and *Ophiopogon.* Lily turf. Evergreen perennials. Hardiness varies. Sun in mild-summer areas, partial or full shade in hot-summer areas. Plants form clumps of narrow leaves resembling coarse grass. Some spread by underground runners and solidly fill in an area; clumping kinds can be planted close for mass effect. All bear small white, lilac, or violet flowers in spikelike clusters. Creeping types include *L. spicata* (creeping lily turf), hardy to –20°F/–29°C, and *O. japonicus* (mondo grass), hardy to 10°F/–12°C, both about 8 inches high; *L. muscari* and its varieties (hardy to –10°F/–23°C) are clumping plants 1 to 2 feet tall.

■ *Mahonia.* Evergreen shrubs. Hardy to –20°F/–29°C. Sun in mild-summer areas, partial shade elsewhere. The variety 'Compacta' of Oregon grape (*M. aquifolium;* see page 81) grows only 1½ to 2 feet tall, making a good-looking high ground cover with lustrous, hollylike foliage, yellow flowers, and blue berries. Spreads widely by underground stems. Creeping mahonia *(M. repens)* has dull bluish green leaves turning bronzy in winter, foliage to 3 feet.

■ *Osteospermum fruticosum.* Trailing African daisy. Evergreen perennial. Hardy to 20°F/–7°C. Full sun. Peak bloom in mid-fall through winter, when garden color is otherwise at a low ebb. Each flower is a 2- to 3-inch daisy of purple, white, or purple and white; gray-green, oval leaves are 1 to 4 inches long. Fast-growing plants may reach 6 to 12 inches; stems root as they touch the soil. (Illustration on facing page.)

■ *Pachysandra terminalis.* Japanese spurge. Evergreen shrub. Hardy to –30°F/–34°C. Shade, acid soil. Spreads by underground stems to form a handsome, even ground cover—even among shallow-rooted shrubs and trees. Dark green, 4-inch, oval leaves are carried on stems that rise to about 10 inches in shade, 6 inches in partial shade. Tiny, fluffy white flowers top foliage in late spring or early summer. (Illustration on facing page.)

■ *Potentilla tabernaemontanii.* Spring cinquefoil. Evergreen perennial. Hardy to –30°F/–34°C. Partial shade where summers are hot and dry, full sun elsewhere. Strawberrylike plant grows rapidly but is easy to contain. Dense foliage of glossy, five-leaflet leaves, spread by runners, builds to about 6 inches high. In spring, ¼-inch yellow flowers dot the surface. Shear or mow to even up surface.

■ *Teucrium chamaedrys.* Germander. Evergreen shrubby perennial. Hardy to –10°F/–23°C. The traditional herb garden border plant thrives in sun or partial shade, even with poor soil and infrequent watering. Spreading stems and ascending branches to about 1 foot tall are clothed with oval, glossy, ½- to 1-inch dark green tooth-edged leaves with prominent veining. Short spikes of small rose-purple flowers (white in one form) appear in summer. Shear back straggly plants. (Illustration on facing page.)

Preparation & Maintenance

All good-looking gardens stem from thoughtful planning, careful preparation, and timely care. These last pages are intended to acquaint you with the preparation and maintenance that go into establishing and keeping up just such an attractive outdoor domain. Though the whole package could be headed "work," remember that you're only dealing with a small space—and for that reason, you may well be able to devote a little extra care to preparing the soil and planting beds.

Your Garden Soil

What looks like plain old garden dirt is actually a complex, dynamic aggregate of mineral particles, organic matter, water, air, and microorganisms. Though a multitude of soil types exist, gardeners usually speak of just three: clay, sand, and loam. It's rare to find a garden soil that's purely one kind or the other, but the soil in your yard probably comes closer to matching one of these types than the other two. It's important to know your soil's character—once you do, you'll also know how best to prepare the ground for planting and how to water it efficiently, and you'll be able to select plants wisely.

Clay soil. This dense soil contains very fine, flattened particles that pack together tightly, leaving little space for air and water. Clay absorbs water slowly and retains it well—so well, in fact, that it generally drains poorly. It also holds dissolved nutrients longer than other soils do, one reason why many clay soils are quite fertile.

Clay is typically sticky when wet, crusty and cracked on the surface when dry. To test for a clay-like soil, shape a handful of moist soil into a ball. Clay will feel slippery; when you release your grip, it will hold together, and if you squeeze it, it will ooze through your fingers in ribbons.

Sandy soil. The opposite of clay, sandy soil is composed of large, rounded particles that pack together loosely, allowing free passage of water and air. Water percolates through quickly, taking dissolved nutrients with it, so plants grown in sandy soil usually need supplemental nutrients and water more often than they would in another soil.

Sandy soil feels gritty rather than sticky. If you squeeze a handful into a ball, it will fall apart when you give it a slight prod—or even as soon as you release your grip.

Loam soil. Somewhere between clay and sand, loam contains organic matter and a mixture of clay, sand, and intermediate-sized silt particles. Water and air move through it slowly enough to keep plant roots moist and nutrients available, but not so slowly as to hamper root development or health.

Loam soils feel less sticky than clay, not as gritty as sand. A handful of moist loam will form a pliable ball that breaks apart with a gentle prod.

Acidity & Alkalinity

Gardeners of yesteryear spoke of soils being sweet (alkaline) or sour (acid). Today, this difference is precisely expressed in pH numbers on a scale of 1 to 14, with the midpoint (pH 7) representing neutral. Soil is acid below pH 7, alkaline (sometimes called *basic*) above pH 7. Acid soil is most common in high-rainfall areas, alkaline soil in regions where rainfall is light. The alkalinity results from a high concentration of calcium carbonate (lime) or certain other minerals such as sodium.

Most popular garden plants perform best over a pH range from slightly acid to neutral (pH 6.5 to 7) and will even prosper in slightly alkaline soil. But certain plants are more particular; heaths, heathers, and rhododendrons, for example, need acid soil for good growth. For this reason, it's a good idea to know your soil's pH; you can have an analysis run by a professional laboratory or test it yourself (with slightly less precise results), using a kit sold at a nursery or garden center. If you need to raise or lower the soil's pH, check with your state or county agricultural extension office for advice.

Drainage

The movement of water downward through soil—drainage—is typically rapid in sandy soils, slow in clay. Furthermore, a given amount of water penetrates about three times deeper in sand than in clay. To moisten a clay soil to the same depth as a sandy one, you'll need about three times as much water; but you won't need to water as often, since clay dries much more slowly than sand.

To find out how well your soil drains, dig a 2-foot-deep hole and fill it with water. When that water has been absorbed, refill the hole and note how long it takes the water to soak in completely. If water remains in the hole after 6 hours, you can assume that drainage is poor. Drainage problems may stem from any of several conditions.

■ *Deep clay soil* almost always drains poorly. To remedy the situation, mix in plenty of organic matter (see facing page). Set out plants on mounds a few inches above the soil grade, then mulch liberally in between. Don't overwater: let the top 2 to 3 inches of soil dry out between waterings.

■ *Compacted soil* is often a problem at new home-sites, thanks to the constant coming and going of heavy equipment. This soil is not only poorly drained, but also difficult to dig and virtually impossible for plant roots to penetrate. The only remedy may be soil-loosening by a landscape contractor using special equipment.

■ *Hardpan*—an impervious layer of soil beneath the surface—will halt drainage even if the top layer of soil is permeable. If the hardpan is fairly thin and close to the surface, you may be able to dig planting holes through it into more porous subsoil (make the holes at least 1 foot in diameter). Otherwise, your best bet is to plant in raised beds filled with good soil (see pages 18–19).

Preparing & Improving Soil

Before setting out the plants in your garden, prepare and amend the soil to get everything off to the best possible start. If you're dealing with a raw site, dig or rotary-till the entire area to break up the soil and clear out any hidden debris; you may also encounter compacted soil (see above). If you're doing an existing garden, construction debris shouldn't be a problem, but you'll still want to dig or till all cleared soil and rid it of any stumps or roots.

Even "good" soils usually can be improved. Nearly all soils, for example, benefit from the addition of organic matter—the decaying remains of plants and animals. This material renders clay soils more permeable and sandy ones more retentive, and helps maintain loam in good condition. Homemade compost is a classic soil amendment—and still one of the best.

Many organic amendments are sold at nurseries and garden centers, packaged in large bags or bales. Look for nitrogen-stabilized wood by-products (shredded bark or aged sawdust), peat moss, animal manures, and commercially prepared composts. You can buy some materials in bulk by the cubic yard—look in the Yellow Pages under Soil Conditioners or Landscape Equipment and Supplies.

Regardless of your soil type, a good rule of thumb is to incorporate a 3-inch layer of organic matter into the upper 8 to 9 inches of soil. Spread the material over the prepared ground, then thoroughly dig or till it in. Figure that 2 cubic feet of organic material will put a 3-inch layer over 9 square feet of soil; 1 cubic yard will cover 108 square feet.

Garden Recycling for Richer Soil

Making compost doesn't have to be a space-gobbling proposition. In Sunset's own test garden, garden refuse is recycled into dark, rich compost in the compact triple-decker bin shown at right.

The three 30-inch-square, 16-inch-high frames were constructed from 2 by 2s joined with L brackets; you could change the size to suit your space. For air circulation, sides were screened with ½-inch wire mesh.

To start compost, garden debris is piled into the bottom section in a 4-inch layer (a shredder first reduces the biggest clippings to speed up the process). The pile is covered with kitchen scraps and manure (a handful of ammonium sulfate could be substituted). Layers are repeated until compost is a few inches above the top of the middle section.

After a week, the compost is turned by inverting the tower. Fresh debris is piled alongside, the top bin is placed around it, and kitchen scraps and manure are added. Then the unfinished compost from the middle section is shoveled onto the pile and the middle frame is moved to the new stack. Finally the contents of the old stack's base are added, and the emptied bin becomes the new top section.

When the top compost level has started to settle into the middle section in a week or two, the pile is ready to be turned again. Usable compost is sifted through the composter's mesh lid (not shown); large pieces are returned to the bin.

Weekly watering keeps the pile about as moist as a squeezed sponge. Bricks under the corners of the bottom bin keep air circulating.

The soil organisms that break down organic materials need nitrogen to thrive. If they can't get it from the organic matter itself, they'll draw upon any available nitrogen in the soil—stealing it, in effect, from plant roots. This can result in temporary nitrogen depletion and reduced plant growth. If you use raw (noncomposted) materials, especially wood products, you'll have to add nitrogen to the soil. Before tilling the raw material into the ground, scatter it with ammonium sulfate, using 1 pound for each 1-inch-deep layer of organic matter spread over 100 square feet. A year later, apply half the initial amount of ammonium sulfate over the area; in the third year, use a quarter as much.

When you add organic amendments to your soil, you can also add fertilizer; a soil test (see "Acidity & Alkalinity," page 88) can tell you what's needed. Of the three major nutrients—nitrogen, phosphorus, and potassium—only nitrogen is water soluble; it can be applied to soil at any time simply by scattering it over the surface. Phosphorus and potassium are essentially insoluble; to be of any value, they must be mixed in at the root zone. Sprinkle them over the soil, then till them in along with the organic amendments.

When you set out trees, shrubs, or vines from 1-gallon or larger containers in an existing garden, you won't be able to improve the soil over a large area. If the soil is sandy to sandy loam, add organic matter to the soil you'll be returning to the planting hole—one part amendment to two parts garden soil. In heavier, more claylike soils, though, return the soil unamended to the planting hole; amended backfill would absorb water more rapidly than the surrounding clay, stay wet longer, and possibly drown plant roots. In such clay soils, the wisest course is to maintain an organic mulch around your plants; as it breaks down, it will gradually improve the upper layer of soil.

Planting Guidelines

In retail nurseries and garden centers, you'll find perennials, annuals, and some ground covers in cell-packs, flats, small pots, and sometimes 1- or 2-gallon containers. Trees, shrubs, and vines will be in containers, from 1-gallon cans on up to boxed mature specimens. Many plants sold by mail-order nurseries are container-grown; for shipping, they're simply removed from their pots and sent off with roots growing in the container soil mix. The illustrations below show appropriate planting methods.

The best time to set out woody plants and perennials varies by region: your aim is to give roots the longest possible period to become established before weather extremes put plants under stress. Summer is the least desirable planting time

Starting Small

Annuals, many perennials, and ground covers are sold in plastic cell-packs or individual small pots. To plant, first remove any matted roots at bottom. Set out plants in prepared soil in holes just deep enough so tops of root balls are even with surface. Fill in with soil and water thoroughly.

Planting from Containers

Dig hole with solid soil base for root ball; top of root ball after planting should be about 2 inches above surrounding soil. Loosen roots, spread them out into hole, and fill in with soil. Mound soil firmly around hole to make watering moat, then water thoroughly.

in all but cool-summer areas, since hot weather puts extra strain on new plants.

Where winters are mild, fall and winter are the best planting seasons; roots grow during the cool weather, so plants are ready for vigorous growth when warmer conditions arrive. In cold-winter areas where soil freezes and snow is the norm, set out most plants in early spring, as soon as the soil can be worked. (For certain perennials, summer is the preferred planting time in these regions.) In low- and intermediate-elevation deserts, plant just as soon as cool weather sets in.

For annuals and vegetables, planting times are more precise.

Watering Systems

Though it's possible to water a small garden by hand or drag a hose and sprinkler around to achieve total coverage, using some sort of water-delivery system is simpler and more effective. Whether you opt for a semipermanent aboveground drip-irrigation system or permanent underground lines, you'll be able to position water-delivery heads for thorough coverage with little or no water waste.

Underground, rigid-pipe systems rely upon high water pressure and volume to distribute water over large areas. In contrast, drip irrigation systems deliver water through flexible tubing at low pressure and volume. Penetration of water into soil is slow; you control the depth by how long you leave the system on. Their flexibility and ease of installation make drip systems especially suitable for small gardens.

Drip Irrigation

You can tailor a drip system to water individual plants with one or more emitters, or you can water larger areas with minisprinklers or minisprayers. You can connect a drip system to a hose end for manual control or make a permanent connection to your main water source; in either case, the system can be run by an automatic controller (see page 93). And since drip lines are on the soil surface (though they can be concealed with mulch or plantings), you can easily change the layout as needed.

Drip emitters are manufactured to deliver specific amounts of water (measured in gallons per hour). Taking into account the emitters' delivery rates and your soil type, you can easily figure out how long the system must run to soak the ground to the depth your plants require. There's no need to make allowances for runoff or evaporation; drip systems waste little or no water in this way.

Components. Drip systems have two basic components—tubing and emitters.

Bare-root Beginnings

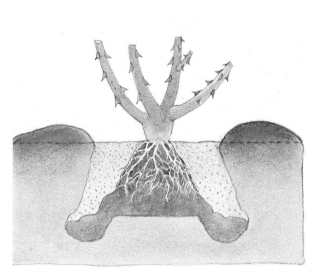

Dig hole with elevated, solid base, then firm a cone of soil nearly to surface level. Spread roots over cone, position plant at proper depth, then add soil, firming as you fill. Mound soil around hole to make watering moat, and water thoroughly. If settling occurs, pump plant up and down to raise while soil is wet.

Balled-and-burlapped Plants

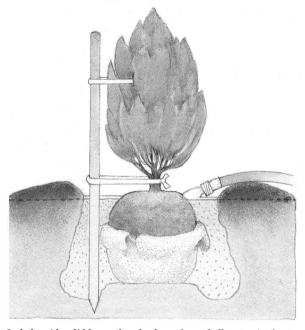

In hole with solid base, place burlapped root ball so top is about 2 inches above surrounding soil. Insert stake beside root ball, partially unwrap burlap (remove entirely if made of synthetic, non-degradable material), and return soil to hole. Form watering moat, thoroughly water, then loosely tie plant to stake.

Water Snake

Lateral line of ⅜-inch drip irrigation tubing snakes around plants, held by hairpin metal stakes. Emitters are added by punching holes, as shown. Tubing can be hidden under mulch.

■ *Tubing.* The main feeder lines are ½- or ⅜-inch black polyethylene tubing; a full range of connectors—elbows, tees, and so on—are available just for assembling the lines into more complex configurations. Quarter-inch microtubing ("spaghetti tubing") can run from the main lines to individual plants. All the tubing is easily cut with scissors or shears; special tools make small holes in the main lines for connecting the microtubing. End caps or closure rings close off each feeder line.

■ *Emitters and sprayers.* You can choose from a wide assortment of emitters, all designed to let water ooze or trickle through small openings at low flow rates. Fit the emitters directly into the main tubing or into the ends of microtubing; certain types ("in-line" emitters) can be made into chains connected by microtubing.

Drip emitters are the best choice for watering individual plants and containers. Some are pressure-compensating, providing a steady flow regardless of fluctuations in water pressure. Minisprayers and minisprinklers spread water over a wider area; they can be installed directly on the main feeder line or elevated on special stakes. Minisprayers are available in spray patterns from partial to full circle, while minisprinklers give only full-circle coverage and emit larger droplets (less affected by wind).

Further essentials. You'll also need a few other items for your drip system.

■ *Valve.* A valve is required to turn the water on and off. If your system operates from the hose end or hose bib, the valve is simply the hose bib; for a system permanently connected to your main water line, you'll need the control and antisiphon valves described below for rigid-pipe systems.

■ *Filter.* To avoid the frustrating chore of cleaning clogged emitters, minisprayers, or minisprinklers, install a good filter between the water source and the system. An in-line filter will service a hose end– or hose bib–operated system; for a permanently connected system, use a Y filter which can be cleaned without disrupting the setup.

■ *Pressure regulator.* Drip irrigation components function best at water pressures between 20 and 30 pounds per square inch—lower than most household water lines. To ensure good performance, most drip systems need a pressure regulator (preset to 20 or 30 psi) to reduce line pressure.

Assembly. To connect your system directly to a main water source, install the components in this order: control valve, antisiphon valve (or combined antisiphon control valve), filter, pressure regulator, and main-line tubing. For connecting to a hose bib, attach the filter to the bib, then the pressure regulator to the filter; follow with the drip tubing. If you're planning to run the system from a hose end, attach the hose after the pressure regulator, then connect the drip line to the end of the hose.

Underground Rigid-pipe Systems

Today's rigid-pipe watering systems are truly permanent, since modern plastic pipe doesn't deteriorate over time as metal pipe does. For lawn maintenance, such systems are your only choice—unless you have a small patch of grass that can be handled by minisprayers on a perimeter drip system.

You can design and install a rigid-pipe system yourself with no special tools or skills, or you can hire a professional (check with a landscape contractor, or look in the Yellow Pages under Sprinklers—Garden and Lawn, Installation and Service). If you do the job yourself, be sure your water supply can run the system you devise. You'll need to know your water pressure, the volume it will deliver (in gallons per minute), and the delivery rates of the sprinkler heads you choose. If a proposed system's output exceeds the supply capacity, you'll have to break the system into two or more circuits.

Components. Between your main water line and the sprinkler system pipes, you'll need a control valve (to regulate the flow from the main water source) and an antisiphon valve or vacuum breaker (to prevent backflow into the main lines). You can buy these combined into one antisiphon control valve.

For pipes and fittings, the best material is polyvinyl chloride (PVC): it won't degrade, it's easily cut, and the pieces can be connected with special PVC solvent cement. If your soil freezes in winter, install copper pipe from the water meter to the control valves, then use PVC pipe. Place an automatic drain valve at the low point of each circuit to keep water from freezing and bursting pipes.

Traditional sprinkler heads deliver fountains of water in full, half, or quarter circles; also available today are heads with rectangular spray patterns and several specialty models. The familiar fountain-spray heads have one chief drawback: they may apply water faster than the soil can absorb it. You can prevent or minimize runoff by watering in a series of short periods, but a simpler solution is to install low precipitation–rate heads.

To provide even coverage, overlap spray patterns; a workable rule is to separate the heads by half the diameter of their coverage. For trees and shrubs with watering basins, bubbler heads produce a reduced flow of water that oozes onto the soil.

Automatic Watering Aids

For either a drip or rigid-pipe system, you can program an electronic controller ("timer") to turn the water on and off. Multiprogram models can even operate a number of different circuits at different frequencies and durations.

The one disadvantage of programmed automatic controllers is that they'll turn water on even if soil is still moist from rain or cool weather. You can use an electronic soil moisture sensor to cue the controller to operate only when soil is dry. A rain shutoff is useful, too; it prevents automatic watering when a certain amount of rain accumulates in a collecting pan.

Garden Maintenance

Though no garden is free from the need for upkeep, the maintenance demands of a small garden are correspondingly modest. The most important advice is simply this: do the job regularly. While a large garden will usually forgive some inattention, ragged edges really show up in a small space. Establish a maintenance schedule; you may well make the pleasant discovery that your monthly care regimen takes no more time than reading one Sunday's newspaper.

Start by asking yourself two questions: What needs to be done? How often must I do it? For each month, rough out a list of tasks and note the anticipated frequency of each. Use this list as the foundation for your working schedule, refining it as you go.

Basic Regular Maintenance

Two jobs loom largest on the regular-maintenance list: watering and grooming.

Rare is the garden of any size that doesn't require watering more often than any other kind of care. Even drought-tolerant plants need periodic watering until their roots are established. To simplify your watering regime, consider installing an irrigation system.

Where grooming is concerned, the amount required depends on what's in your garden. If you have a lawn, for example, the most pressing tasks will surely be mowing and edging. Usually ranking second to lawn care is general tidying-up, including blowing, raking, or hosing paved surfaces to clear them of litter. As your garden blossoms (and possibly bears fruit), you'll also want to clip off spent flowers and pick up any fallen fruits. To minimize future work, carry a pair of pruning shears as you make your rounds during the growing season; nip off wayward growth before it develops into a pruning job.

Weed control may or may not be on your list of "regulars," depending upon whether or not you use any of the control measures outlined below.

Periodic Maintenance

Beyond the regular upkeep, you'll need to concern yourself with a few other, less frequent tasks.

Planting. Annual crops, whether ornamental or edible, need timely planting preceded by some soil preparation (see page 89). Be sure to set out each type of plant at the start of its growing period.

Many perennial flowers must be dug, divided, and replanted in rejuvenated soil every few years or so. Check the descriptions of your particular plants to see how often.

Mulching. Good gardeners have long realized the benefits of mulching—topping the soil with an insulating layer of loose organic matter one to several inches thick. A mulch keeps soil cooler and damper during hot weather, since moisture from watering is retained longer. And as the organic material breaks down, it improves the upper layer of soil, allowing easier penetration by water and roots.

Mulching also aids in weed control: seeds are effectively "buried" and cannot germinate. Any weeds that do sprout are easy to root out, thanks to the mulch's loose structure.

There's a wide choice of suitable mulch materials. Remember, though, that the mulch you choose must be fairly loose and permeable to water; avoid thin-textured leaves, thickly piled lawn clippings, and any other material that tends to pack down into an impenetrable mat.

Gardening on the Rocks

If you worry that a small garden will limit your ability to grow a great number of different plants, investigate the world of rock gardening.

Rock gardens are more than simply gardens with rocks. In the original sense, they were "alpine gardens" where European plant connoisseurs tried to raise the choice, small high-mountain species found above the timberline. These gardeners attempted to recreate in miniature the rocky and pebble-strewn homelands of alpine plants, complete with contrived screes and moraines.

The Japanese developed another rock garden style, capturing greatly reduced renditions of natural landscapes (often rocky) in home gardens. Plants are correspondingly small in scale, though they're not necessarily high-mountain denizens. Symbolism is important: rock placements may not so much replicate natural arrangements as represent natural forms. A single large rock, for example, might stand for a mountain.

Contemporary rock gardens usually borrow from both European and Japanese traditions, perhaps employing a bit of mountainous-looking rock but using small plants from other-than-alpine habitats.

At its tiniest, a rock garden can be a display of alpine or small plants in a modest container. A step up in size is the classic English "trough garden," originally planted in old stone watering troughs; you can use an imitation stone trough constructed from cement and peat moss, or a sturdy wooden planter. A sunny raised bed can easily become a rock garden, as can a dry-laid stone retaining wall—just tuck suitable plants into niches of soil between the stones.

Basic requirements. Whether you will be growing a woodland, desert, or mountain plant assortment, choose

Rock garden in spring displays blue lithodora, yellow achillea, gray-leafed Veronica cinerea, and Armeria juniperifolia in pink and white.

a sunny location with good air circulation. Heavy shade and stagnant air foster diseases such as mildew and root rots.

Grow your rock garden plants in well-drained soil. If you'll be planting in a container or raised bed, a suitable medium can be made from one part good garden soil (not clay), one part builder's or river sand, and one part peat moss or nitrogen-stabilized bark. (For plants that prefer acid soil, use

two parts peat moss or bark to one part each soil and sand.) If you're planning an in-ground rock garden, dig or till an organic amendment (such as nitrogen-stabilized bark) into the top 8 to 10 inches of soil to improve its permeability. In heavier, claylike soils, it's also a good idea to raise the planting beds above the naural grade to ensure good drainage.

If there's no nearby source of free local stone, look in the Yellow Pages under Rock or Landscape Equipment and Supplies. Avoid quarried or broken-up rocks, since their jagged, unweathered surfaces always appear unnatural. And don't overlook artificial stone; some is virtually impossible to tell from the genuine item.

A selection of plants. The following plants will turn in rewarding performances wherever they are adapted.

■ **Perennials**—*Achillea tomentosa, Aethionema, Alyssum montanum, Anacyclus depressus, Arabis, Armeria, Aubrieta deltoidea, Dianthus* (some), *Dryas, Echeveria, Erodium chamaedryoides, Festuca ovina glauca, Geranium argenteum, G. cinereum, Iberis sempervirens, Iris cristata, Oenothera missourensis, Origanum dictamnus, Phlox subulata, Potentilla cinerea, Primula* (many), *Saxifraga, Sedum* (many), *Sempervivum, Silene acaulis, Thymus, Veronica* (several).

■ **Bulbs**—*Crocus, Cyclamen, Fritillaria meleagris, Iris reticulata, Narcissus bulbocodium, N. cyclamineus, N. triandrus, Oxalis adenophylla, O. hirta.*

■ **Shrubs**—*Andromeda polifolia, Berberis stenophylla* 'Corallina Compacta', *B. thunbergii* 'Crimson Pygmy', *Calluna vulgaris* (some), *Daphne* (some), *Erica* (some), *Hebe cupressoides* 'Nana', *Hypericum coris, Jasminum parkeri, Rhododendron* (smallest species).

Suitable packaged mulches, widely available at nurseries and garden centers, include wood products (such as bark chips, shredded bark, and nitrogen-fortified sawdust), animal manures, and commercial composts. Landscape supply outlets sometimes sell materials in bulk, particularly by-products of regional commerce—various wood by-products, mushroom compost, apple or grape pomace, ground corncobs, and more. If you use wood by-products, you may need to take steps to prevent nitrogen depletion; see "Preparing & Improving Soil," page 89. Good mulches can also be found in your own neighborhood; you may be able to gather pine needles or oak leaves, for example. And if you have room for a compost pile, you'll have a constant mulch supply.

Mulch is best applied after the soil has warmed in spring. Pull or hoe any large weeds, but count on the mulch to smother most weed seedlings. Because mulch decomposes over time, it's a good idea to replenish it annually.

Weed control. Weeds are especially noticeable in a restricted space. Fortunately, they are also easier to vanquish in a small garden. Whatever method you use, timing is the key: get the weeds before they go to seed. If you break the cycle of seeding, you'll have to contend only with weeds from seeds carried in by wind, birds, and muddy feet.

Before an area is planted, tilling is the simplest way to clear out annual weeds. (Hoeing is as effective, but harder on the muscles.) Perennial weeds such as dandelions are better dealt with by hand, so that you can be sure you've removed all roots. Once the garden has been planted, hand pulling is the surest control, with hoeing a close second if there's room to avoid annihilating desirable plants.

After your garden is cleared of weeds, a mulch offers effective control. In beds of established plants, you can also apply a preemergence herbicide to kill weeds just as they germinate. Apply the herbicide to tilled soil *before* you expect the weeds to germinate, then water it in. The label will tell you which weeds each product controls and on which plants it can be used safely; follow all directions to the letter.

In some situations—weeds growing in pavement, for example—a contact herbicide is the easiest solution. Products containing glyphosate are particularly effective on hard-to-dig perennial weeds, but don't let any droplets fall on desirable plants. Nontoxic contact herbicides containing fatty acids kill weeds on contact by burning and rupturing their tissues. These, too, should be used with extreme care, but they're less likely to do lasting damage to any accidentally-sprayed plants.

Fertilizing. The need to fertilize is determined by the plants you grow and the sort of soil in your gar-den (see page 88). Of the three major plant nutrients, nitrogen (responsible for vigorous growth and bloom) is the most important. Because it's water-soluble, it's also the most easily depleted—and the easiest to add at any time. Phosphorus and potassium are virtually insoluble, so fertilizers containing these nutrients do the most good if dug into the soil within the root zone.

Check the descriptions of your plants to determine their needs. Many common trees and shrubs will prosper year after year with no fertilizer at all, so feeding these plants is a waste of time and money. Certain popular shrubs, though, do benefit from periodic fertilizing. Camellias and azaleas, for example, may enjoy healthier growth and heavier flowering with an annual fertilizer application.

Perennial plants generally prosper from fertilizer applied just as active growth begins. To enhance the following year's growth, some gardeners also give plants a dose after flowering has finished.

For annuals and vegetables, soil amended and fertilized before planting (see pages 89–90) may provide enough nutrients. But some growers fertilize during the blooming (and bearing) season to promote more and larger flowers and produce.

Pest and disease control. The mere presence of a pest or disease in your garden shouldn't have you hauling out the heavy artillery. Learn to distinguish between casual and significant damage—and accept the casual sort, realizing that most pests have natural enemies to keep them in check. Promiscuous use of controls can kill these helpful natural enemies as well, almost guaranteeing a greater problem the next time around.

If you notice an unusually heavy pest infestation, though, or a disease that's spreading, the time for tolerance is past. First try mechanical methods: hand-picking, setting out various traps and barriers, and hosing to wash off and kill pests. If you plan to spray, consider using nonchemical preparations such as insecticidal soaps, botanical insecticides (pyrethrins, for example), horticultural oils, and—for caterpillars—*Bacillus thuringiensis* (BT).

In some situations, stronger chemical remedies are in order; they're often needed to deal with diseases and spider mite infestations, for example. Choose a control that is effective against the specific problem and be sure to observe *all* cautions and directions on the product label.

Pruning. Some garden plants—roses are a classic example—can profit from regular annual pruning, with occasional clipping during the growing season. Other spring- and summer-flowering shrubs, some vines, and a few trees may need periodic thinning of weak, superfluous, or dead wood.

To keep major pruning to a minimum, regularly clip off errant growth that, if left to follow its own inclinations, might have to be pruned later on.

Index